Shim,

His Puppet
NO MORE!

Thank you FOR
Your Support.

Leni Romano
9-2015

Editor:
Joseph Henderson, BA, MFA
BA, English Major
MFA in Writing,
Current Manuscripts:
"Being Human" (a full length book of poetry)
"What I Remember" (a Chapbook)

Book Cover and Logo Designed by:
Tom Messina
Total Concept, Inc.
Fort Myers, Florida
www.totalconcept.com

ISBN: 145282701X
ISBN-13: 9781452827018
Library of Congress Control Number: 2010905762

His Puppet
NO MORE!

by
RENA ROMANO
a memoir

To the love of my life, my husband David, thank you for your patience, endless love, and loyal support. Your strength keeps me going. Thank you for sticking with me during my journey, especially during my dark hours. I love you madly.

To Butchy and Karl, my wonderful brothers, thank you for your constant support and encouragement. But most of all, thank you for loving me the way brother's should love their sister.

*I want to thank my wonderful Cousin
Joseph for believing in me.
Thank you for your love and support,
and helping me put my memories on paper.*

*There are good men in the world and
I thank all of you for proving that to me.*

To my sister Punkin and sister in-law Carol who always loved me, but didn't understand my struggle, thank you both for being there for me. I love you very much.

To my friend Gillian, thank you.

To Mom and Donna, I love and miss you both.

This is my story of incest and childhood sexual abuse as I remember living through it. My brothers and sister have given me their verbal permission and blessing to share their stories with you. My friends and other family members mentioned by their first names have given me written permission to use their names and stories and share with you, as I remember their stories told to me. I thank each and every one of you for your support. You've been with me on my journey as I reclaimed my life and I love you all dearly.

RENA ROMANO
a memoir

CONTENTS

Part One

His Puppet

Part Two

NO MORE!

PREFACE

I have been writing and rewriting this book for the last eighteen years or so. But not until this moment not a single word, not a sentence of my past, was written on paper. It was in my head, neatly filed away in my brain. Only during still moments or if something triggered a memory, would I bring those memories out and compose a new line or start a new chapter, but only in my head. After completing almost two years of intense group therapy for childhood abuse, I had this insatiable desire to write about what happened to me. I felt if I could overcome the years of differing abuses I endured, if I could be a survivor of child abuse, possibly, hopefully, my story could help others.

Silently relieved, soon after therapy my desire to write this book was put on hold. I had an excuse I have used these past years to postpone sharing my story. I knew once I started putting my words on paper I would be enduring the pain of losing a loved one. Now that I am sitting here typing, this could only mean one dreadful thing: I traded its birth for a death. Sitting by my mother's side wiping the last tear from her eye, telling her it was ok to go, I watched her peacefully pass away.

It had been almost a year since her passing and I was still looking for excuses to avoid writing. Not only did I lose my mother that year, but also, two months before her death I lost my younger sister to breast cancer. Earlier in the year my brother-in-law died as well. Cancer took three members of my family that year. 2006 really sucked!! Two days after my mother passed away I was laid off from work. I welcomed being unemployed. I was surrounded by so much death I just needed room to breathe. I could not emotionally handle grieving, writing about the child abuse I had endured, and work at the same time.

A few months after Mom passed away I started saying to my husband perhaps I would start working on my book. I asked him several times if he could handle all the horrific little details I would write about and he assured me he could. He said, *"Go for it."* I still had not shared with him in great detail what happened to me. I didn't need to and I don't think he really wanted to hear it all. Just knowing the abuse happened makes him more than furious. I kept hoping he would say it would bother him so that, consequently, I would have another excuse. Fortunately I married a man who is very self-assured. His self-esteem is the strongest I have ever seen.

My husband kept encouraging me to write and he would often comment, *"You might be surprised during the process, you might have a huge revelation."* But he was wrong. I had many revelations along the way. I had to stop writing, walk away from it, to cry and grieve for the little girl that had her life stolen from her. Once I felt strong enough I would begin writing again, and I couldn't type fast enough. It was like an oil-spill gushing from a broken tanker flooding onto paper.

This book is a story of horrors. But it is also a book of new possibilities. I thought I didn't want pity for what happened to me, but it turned out that was exactly what I wanted. I was stuck playing the victim of abuse. I thought I was motivated to write my story to help others, but I came to realize I was motivated out of selfishness. In constant motion but not going anywhere, not changing my life, I was stuck like a rat in a spinning wheel. I truly wanted pity from the world and I wanted to be right about the wrongs that were forced upon me. I had long ago accepted what happened to me but I still held on to the abuse, I could not leave it where it was, in the past.

I kept the past abuses with me in the present and in doing so they were keeping me from my life and my future. I have come to understand the disingenuous life I was living. The process of writing has been a journey. I have taken the ride of my life. At times it has been excruciatingly painful but at other times completely exhilarating. I have gained a profound understanding of my life with the help of numerous people from all walks of life, from around the world. I was given the wisdom to know the difference between motivation and inspiration: to be inspired is selfless and the rewards will have a greater purpose. I am now inspired to share my story with others. That is what I genuinely wanted and I will be forever grateful to those people who helped me see the distinction between the two.

I want to share my story and my greatest desire in doing so is that others will seek help for the childhood abuse they have endured. My sincere hope is that other victims of child abuse can learn from what I am writing and understand they too can leave their abuse in the past where it belongs and embrace the endless possibilities of whatever life they want to have. Any form of child abuse is damaging to the soul. Those of us who have been a victim of abuse must reclaim our lives and the very essence of our being. We must take back what was stolen from us by those who murdered our innocence. It is our life. It is our right to choose our own destiny. Every victim of any form of child abuse must stand firm and refuse to let our abusers or our past control us any longer.

"I cannot change what happened to me but I can change how it controlled my life. I did not choose to be abused but I choose to soar above it."

INTRODUCTION

"Three may keep a secret, if two of them are dead."
Benjamin Franklin (1706 - 1790)

Every family has its secrets and my family was no exception. My secrets became entangled webs of deception, and were completely infested with the discarded remains of the lies I had to tell through the years because I could never speak the truth. My secrets were so horrendous I believe Satan himself might have trouble spewing them from his hideous lips. Everyone in my family had secrets: Mom, my brothers, my sisters, and I. We were unable to share our secrets with each other and, unthinkably, the outside world. From the outside looking in it appeared we weren't any different than our neighbors. Or were we? Some family secrets are never told and are buried with their victim or the perpetrator. I can only speculate if I am alone, or are there others like me? Are there other people harboring secrets such as mine? I didn't believe there were any for the longest time. My secrets were so unbearable, so unspeakable, surely no one else had secrets as shocking as mine. I couldn't tell anyone for many, many, years, I was THAT ashamed.

In fact, it would take over thirty years before I ever uttered one word of my secrets. I couldn't, it was too painful, too shameful to think or talk about. I always knew what happened to me, but I didn't realize how much my secrets controlled me. Their hold on me was tighter than a vise. Every waking moment, every breath I took, the unspeakable was in control. It was as though my invisible life parachute failed to open and I was spiraling out of control, plummeting into the unimaginable deepest depths of hell. Some people suppress the memories of what happened to them as children. I thought I only suppressed the pain: the pain of what was done to me both during the abuse, and for many years afterward. Fortunately I was able to recognize the only way to recovery, the only way to release the unshakable grip my secrets had on me and gain control of my life, would be through professional therapy.

Once I found the right setting the healing process could begin. I came to realize, unfortunately, there are others out there like me, millions of them, women and men, and they too have unspeakable family secrets. I found a support group I was comfortable with. There were six other women and two therapists in that group. Once I started sharing my dark secrets and the others began to share theirs, I knew I found the right place to heal. It was ok to talk about what happened to us. It was a safe place and no one could hurt us there. It was exhausting, it was excruciating but the only way to be free from the suffering caused by our secrets was to talk about them. I came to understand I SHOULD NOT feel ashamed or blame myself for what others forced upon me for so many years as a child.

After I finished with group therapy in 1992, I told my mother my desire to write a book about the child abuse I endured for many years. I told her my need to share with others how I was able to forgive myself and stop abusing myself for what others had done to me. I want to speak publically to other victims and encourage them to seek help. I want to scream with joy from the mountains tops that we can be more than just survivors. We can learn to take our lives back and, most profoundly, triumph over the abuse.

Mom was a tall woman, five foot ten. You could sense her height even sitting in a chair. She always sat upright and proud: head high, legs crossed, an elbow on the arm of the chair looking out as if her subjects were bowing before her. The moment I told her my intentions to write a book, I could see the pain in her eyes. Suddenly she looked very small, like a rag doll that had been carelessly tossed in the corner of an overstuffed chair. Her arms and legs went life-less and her head dropped. She was too ashamed to show her face and she slumped in the chair. Her comfortable, quiet, world as she knew it was about to be turned upside down for the outside world to see and dissect, and it scared the life out of her.

At that moment we switched roles. I became the adult and she turned into the frightened little girl I felt I must protect. I knew part of her fear was for me. I also knew she felt people would blame her for not protecting me. She didn't say it, but I could tell her greatest fear was that if I told my unspeakable secrets, people outside the family would find out about hers: the secrets she carefully and silently carried with her all those years, secrets she desperately wished she could have carried to her grave. Mom was not then, nor would she ever be willing to share any of our family secrets, not one word of them. As strong as my mother appeared to others, there was only one time prior to this moment that I witnessed how fragile she could be. It was years earlier, the night I found out about her darkest secret.

I understood her pain and I could sense the overwhelming emotions that were racing through her mind. Her emotions were so distressing she could not hold them back any longer. They completely overwhelmed her. Covering her face with her hands she started sobbing. It was as if the temperature in the room suddenly dropped below freezing, her body shuddered and she began shaking uncontrollably. She was utterly repulsed by the betrayal of trust by my perpetrators, and consumed with the shame and the guilt for what happened to me. After all, she was the one who had left me in the care of the ones who abused me.

Not once in all of those years did I give her any reason to believe the people she had entrusted me to would be anything other than my protectors. We all kept our secrets hidden so well no one ever had a clue what was truly happening to me. She remembered faintly, years ago, someone telling her she should not let me spend so much time with him: him being the one who was the main perpetrator of my abuse, my first offender and the one who did the most damage to my soul. After I revealed my horrific secrets, my family and friends began to understand why I lived the destructive, self-deprecating, lifestyle I had.

Many times I pleaded with Mom to go to therapy, to talk to someone to help her work through the shame and guilt she was feeling. But as much as I tried I could not convince her she was not the one who should be blamed for any of the abuse that I endured. But she did blame herself. She was furious with herself for not picking up on the comment made so many years ago by a friend and not understanding the insinuation of it. Perhaps she could have saved me. How could she possibly know, *"You shouldn't let her spend so much time with him,"* meant for years my worst offender had thrust himself upon me and forced me to perform the most horrendous, incestuous acts. She felt she was smarter than that, she should have known better and as a mother she felt she let me down. I felt her intense pain, I told her not to worry I would wait on writing my book. At that moment, I secretly made a promise to myself that when she passed away I would share my story with the world.

As the afternoon went on I could see Mom regaining her composure, getting stronger, and becoming more enraged. She hated being emotionally out of control.

She was too stubborn, too proud, to let that happen. She did not like to appear weak in front of her children or anyone for that matter. She was the matriarch and must stay composed. It was as though a board had been suddenly nailed to her back. She sat straight up and lit a cigarette. I joined her. The cigarettes seemed to calm us both down and we started talking. She said, *"Not in a million years did I ever imagine one of my three daughters was a victim of child sexual abuse."* The statistics at that time were one out of every three girls would become a victim of child sexual abuse, and I was the one.

Mom thought all of her children had escaped the ugliness of child abuse. She believed for years the chain of abuse in our family had been broken. There are many forms of child abuse and I don't think she ever realized all six of her children had suffered some form of abuse at the hands of someone else. My mother had been abused. She never admitted to any sexual abuse, but she shared the emotional, verbal, and physical neglect she suffered from her own mother.

My mother was a strong-willed opinionated woman and considered herself a feminist. She was independent, educated, well read and up to date on all current events, not only locally but worldly too. Yet she was still controlled by the beliefs of her time that you did not talk about sexual topics. You did not put your family affairs out on the street, as if in a tabloid, you kept them behind closed doors. During her era, which was WWII, there were no talk shows openly discussing child sexual abuse or rape, or crimes against women. They did not go to therapy or take antidepressants. People of her era "sucked it up" and went about their lives pretending such evil things only happened to other people and that was how she wanted to handle this situation.

The family would learn of my secrets, and that's where Mom wanted to keep them. She could not share them with the world. Mom was happy I sought help through counseling but she was not willing to seek help for herself. I always felt she believed that she didn't deserve to be free from her own pain. She wanted to keep her pain to punish herself. I understood that because I tortured myself for years for the abuse I endured. I felt I deserved to suffer. I believed for the longest time it was my own fault, for what happened to me, and I felt I should be punished.

To be completely honest, I was selfishly relieved to see how much Mom was hurting. Not that I blamed her for what happened but it gave me an excuse to postpone writing my story. Even though I had this overwhelming need to write and share with others what happened, I was petrified at the thought of exposing myself to the world. I still felt an overwhelming shame. Any form of child abuse is horrific but I think incest is the hardest for a victim to accept. Reliving over and over in my mind what happened was one thing, but it was still my secret and I felt safe as long as I held it inside. The thought of putting my memories on paper and sharing them with the world made me feel naked, completely vulnerable. I was in my mid-thirties at the time and I had gone through therapy, but I felt like a scared child taking her first step: emotionally holding on, putting one foot in front of the other, not knowing if I was doing the right thing by wanting to share my story. I realized I still had a lot of healing to do and I needed more time to grow stronger. Plus, I was still harboring another secret.

That summer day so many years ago, the first time the sexual abuse happened, my emotional growth stopped, cut short as if it were hacked off like a young sprouting limb never to reach its full thriving beauty. At thirty-four, finally learning how to live healthy emotionally and physically, I could start to nurture my emotional wounds and I was finally able to start maturing properly. It seemed I was starting over, picking up from that first day, and I was four years old again. I was finally growing up. I had to forgive myself. Just like my mother, I felt others would blame me for what happened. I had taken responsibility for my unwilling involvement, but I wasn't sure how others would view the situation. I never shared that particular fear with my mother or anyone else.

Child abuse in any form is the most horrendous act a human being can inflict upon another human. Many people believe murdering someone is the ultimate sinful act. I'm not so sure I agree. Yes, it is a horrific evil act and we should never commit murder. But I believe when our body dies our souls are set free, and they are at peace for eternity. Our souls are set free from the suffering of our human life. I believe when a child is sexually abused the body remains alive but the spirit is in mortal danger. Over time if the victim does not seek and receive proper help, their spirit can endure a long painful death years before the physical body dies. Long after a perpetrator stops the abuse, victims can become imprisoned into a lifetime of self-abuse: victims roaming the earth searching for their lost souls, all the while victimizing themselves or others. Roaming and searching for years, abusing myself, I could not understand why I continued to make the choices I did to harm myself and sabotage my life. Not until therapy did I understand what I was doing and why. My spirit was slowly being destroyed: at first by my abusers, then later I was committing spiritual suicide through my own actions.

One day, soon after I hit rock bottom, I received a gift. It came in a box. It wasn't a traditional gift box and it wasn't wrapped. Staring at the TV, listening to a female voice, it was as though she was speaking directly to me. She told me it was ok to talk about what happened and seek help. Had I not listened to that voice and reached out for professional help, I would have continued to live in a self-induced nightmare for the rest of my life. I often say, *"When I die I will surely go to heaven because I've already been through hell here on earth."*

Thank God I inherited a lot of my mother's strength. I could always "suck it up" and be strong, or at least appear to be. All of those years I never gave anyone any reason to think that the people I loved were sexually abusing me. I loved them, but mostly I feared them, so I had to keep our secrets. I could have won an Oscar for my years of deception as to what our relationships truly were. However there was one person that intuitively knew and she was almost killed for confronting my worst offender. She tried to save me, but if she told anyone her suspicions of what he was doing he would have either killed her or had her killed. He had to protect our secret. I was his plaything, his puppet, and for years I believed the only way I would be free of his control would be by his decision alone.

After Mom passed away I found two letters she wrote to him. In the beginning of each letter the words are somewhat legible. Her anger is evident by the enraged strokes from the pencil, and the paper almost ripped in half. Half way through the letters her handwriting takes a turn. It becomes shaky in appearance. I can tell she is not pressing down as hard. Farther along in the letters her emotions appear to be more excruciating and some of the words look as if they have dissolved into one another from the tears that apparently dropped on them. The betrayal to the family was completely overwhelming, it seemed the weight of the pencil became too much for her to bear. As if she was lifting a wooden cross between her fingers, struggling, barely able to glide the pencil over the paper, her sentences become incoherent. Some sentences she didn't complete.

Why Mom never mailed the letters to him I will never know. From the moment she found out about the abuse she did not want any connection to him at all. Perhaps by not mailing the letters he would not have a reason to contact her. Maybe it was a form a therapy for her and, possibly, she hoped he would get them after she died. In one letter she wrote that she might be able to forgive him for all the awful things he did to her, but she would never ever be able to forgive him for the horrendous things he did to me. In caps she wrote, "*YOU ARE A SICK, SICK, MAN.*"

For the remainder of my mother's life she kept up the pretense of being strong on the outside, but I knew on the inside she was silently punishing herself. She wanted to keep her pain. She could not let go of it. She felt it was her cross to bear. Mom never forgave herself for the things she did that led to his existence. Her secret had come out long before mine and it tormented her until the day she died. One of the last things she said to me was, "*If I hadn't brought him into our world things might have turned out differently for all of us. Perhaps your life might have been spared from the hellish nightmare you went through for so many years.*"

PART ONE

His Puppet

1

I remember the day he came to our home. It was a pleasant summer day, warm but not scorching hot like most days in Kansas can get. The sky was blue and there were large white clouds of varying shapes and sizes slowly drifting along. There was great excitement in the air, or so I thought. I was told years later it was not excitement but great apprehension that he was coming to our home. I was running around the house barefoot, wearing a tee shirt and shorts. My light brown hair was cut in a pixie style because it was easier for Mom to take care of. I remember dancing about and clapping my chubby little hands as though it was the greatest celebration of the year, even better than Christmas.

I was singing "Dean Dean's coming home, Dean Dean's coming home." He was coming home from where I didn't know, and I didn't care, I was just completely and erroneously filled with joy at the thought of seeing him. I'm not sure but I believe I was the one that coined his nickname, Dean Dean. Later his name became, simply, Dean. At four years old I could not pronounce my G's without a bit of a lisp so the nickname stuck. Dean Dean. All of my brothers and sisters had nicknames. The oldest of Mom's six children, Anna Lee, was nicknamed Punkin, the oldest boy William was called Butch or Butchy. Donna Kay, my younger sister, we called her Donk. The youngest, Karl, got stuck with Boo because he was always hiding and jumping out from his secret places trying to scare us. The older he became, he insisted we call him Karl. I cannot recall why I was nicknamed Reen Ran. Perhaps it was because I was always in motion, running and playing as a happy child does. Years later I would be called the General. It was silly but endearing to call everyone by our nicknames and I still do, all but Dean Dean.

Our new home was a duplex made of concrete cinder blocks. There were rows and rows of cinder block houses, a whole village of them. They were painted white on the outside. I'm sure that was probably the least expensive way to paint all of them. There was no sheetrock or insulation on the inside walls, they were the same cinder block, but you were able to paint the inside any color you wanted.

Mom painted our inside walls a bright sky blue. The buildings reminded me of monopoly pieces, all the same size lined up in a row. Unlike the game of monopoly with its expensive boardwalk, this village was not the least bit glamorous. There were no trees and very little grass, no yards to speak of. The houses were infested with cockroaches and they didn't care what time of day it was they would crawl everywhere. I would smash them with my chubby little hand as they scurried up the walls. Making a game of smashing them I cringed and giggled with a sense of power at destroying them.

The duplexes were built during WWII to house the people who worked at a nearby ammunition plant. They were the bare minimum but livable. After the war they were sold to an investor and he in turn rented the units or sold them through a rent-to-own program. They weren't much to look at but they afforded families with lower incomes to own a small piece of the American dream. It was 1960, and it was all Mom and her new husband Bob could afford at the time. It was a roof over our heads and it gave us more room so Dean could move in with us.

I'm not even sure if I had met Dean before that day. He was a scrawny fifteen year old kid with sandy light brown hair and blue eyes. It's hard to remember exactly what he looked liked, but James Dean, in the movie *Rebel Without a Cause*, comes to mind: hair slicked back, jeans with a white tee shirt with the sleeves rolled up, and a cigarette in his mouth. Dean was rebellious to any authority, the kind of kid your parents warned you not to hang around with.

I was excited to see him come through the door. I screamed with joy running towards him and jumped into his arms. He seemed happy to see me too. As the day went on I think he was glad to have the distraction of playing with me rather than talking with Mom or the other adults. He wanted to avoid, as long as he could, any conversation of his recent unwanted living conditions. He tickled me, we laughed and played, it seemed to go on forever and I wished it had.

Years later I was told Dean spent some time in Juvey (juvenile detention). He was sent there two or three different times between the ages of ten and fifteen. He came home to live with us after an arrangement had been made for his release on the condition Mom would move out of the state of Missouri. That was the third time she was forced to move because of Dean. Dean couldn't live at Grandma Marsh's anymore because she also lived in Missouri and there was nowhere else for the authorities to send him, and no one else would take him. So Mom packed us up and moved us to that cinder block house in Kansas. I'm quite sure if that sleepy little town in Kansas knew what was going to happen they would have pleaded for her not to move there. Dean was a storm to be reckoned with. An F5 tornado was like a mild summer breeze compared to his vicious force. He was a rebel "with" a cause. Everywhere he went he left a path of destruction: theft, vandalism, physical abuse, sexual abuse, lives destroyed, lives lost.

Mom told me one of Dean's stints in Juvey was because he test-drove a car and failed to return it. My older sister, Punkin, told me he showed up at her house with the stolen car and she was the one that turned him in. Mom accepted the blame for his incarceration because she knew if he found out it was Punkin he would have retaliated by either hurting her physically or do something destructive to her property. You were careful not to cross Dean because you would surely pay dearly for it. *"He's a mean son of a bitch,"* Mom said often through the years. He retaliated against my mother time and time again. I think she felt if he were taking things out on her maybe he would leave others alone. He was always stealing her belongings, money, car, or household items that could be pawned. Dean cursed her many times. Once I saw him kick in her car door while she and Punkin were sitting in it. I don't believe he ever hit her, if he had, Butchy would have beat him badly.

I found out later, after therapy, his last stint in Juvey was because he got caught having sex with a neighbor girl, and she was much younger than him. At the time I don't think they considered it sexual abuse. He was just going through puberty, and the only way they knew to control his sexual appetite was to put him in Juvey. Finally, after all those years his secret was out so it made sense. Perhaps the authorities did understand the seriousness of his sexual aggressiveness and that was why Mom was forced to move from Missouri to Kansas. They wanted as much distance as was feasibly possible between him and the girl to prevent it from happening again. I'm sure Mom never anticipated his sexual aggressiveness would turn towards me. Had she any inkling he was capable of incest, I am certain she would have left him in Juvey to rot.

Dean made me feel special with the constant playfulness and attention. Before he moved in with us no one gave me the time or affection I was now receiving from him. I was happy and having fun that someone, anyone, was paying attention to me. I was drawn to his irresistible charm, it felt innocent sweet and safe. The time he spent with me filled my heart with joy. The more attention he gave me the more I craved, and my trust in him grew unequivocally.

Sadly, the sweet innocence I felt in his presence would soon disappear. We were alone playing, laughing, tickling and running around the house. Suddenly, Dean's demeanor changed. He took my hand and led me to the bedroom. I started feeling uneasy as he sat on the corner of the bed. My laughter quickly faded as he unzipped his pants and pulled me towards him.

Standing there looking up at him, my big brown eyes were looking into his trying to understand what he was doing to me. My eyes were questioning his. He could see the fear and confusion in them, but that did not stop him. I trusted him completely, and I remember feeling that what he was making me do to him must be ok, because he said he loved me and continued to assure me that we were having fun. But as he continued I could feel my spirit, my inner-light, start slowly fading away like a dying star trapped by the grasp of a black hole and plummeting deeper into the bowels of its darkness. Even at four years old I was conscious of and could sense the essence of my wholeness being shattered, broken in half. I could feel my happiness slipping away. I became scared, and even though it did not feel natural, I did not pull away from him. I'm not sure why. I completely adored him, and I was afraid to do anything that might disappoint him, so I obediently stood there until he finished.

Dean charmed me with his attention, manipulated me with his words, and then seduced me with his deceptive affection. It was as though he could hypnotize me to submit and I would do whatever he desired of me. Through the years he was skillful at controlling me and made me believe I wanted to do the things I did. I believed I was supposed to pleasure him. Slowly being programmed, I felt I was put upon this earth just for him. I could never say no to him no matter what it was.

When I was older and first tried to say "*NO*" Dean threw a tantrum, screaming, stopping his feet and flailing his arms around like a spoiled child who had his favorite toy taken away as punishment. His face became completely contorted when he threw his tantrums. It was like watching an exorcism as pure evil completely engulfed his body. The first time I witnessed a tantrum I was completely shocked, and he made me feel ashamed for denying him. Many tantrums followed over the years. They frightened me into submission. For years it seemed I had no choice but to do what he demanded. Slowly, year after year, every bit of dignity I had was stripped away. It took a long time before I was emotionally strong enough to tell him to keep his damned hands off of me.

The sexual abuse started in the bedroom, and the emotional-mental abuse was not far ahead. Not long after that day a neighbor boy, my age, and I were playing. We got into the back seat of a car. I don't know how things started I just remember us laughing and it was as innocent as show me yours and I'll show you mine. I didn't think anything sexual about it. I was only four years old so I didn't know what sex was or what inappropriate behavior was between a boy and a girl. I was shown just days before by someone I trusted and loved that pulling your pants down seemed like suitable behavior. We had taken our pants off and we were sitting there giggling and pointing at each other.

Someone spotted us. Then Dean showed up. I don't remember what he said I just remember how terrible I felt by how he was acting. I started crying uncontrollably. I looked at him, confused, thinking "Why are you making me feel so awful when you did the same thing to me?" The message was so mixed and my innocent mind could not even comprehend the complexity of it. The look on his face filled me with humiliation. He could see the shame swelling in my confused brown eyes and he just smirked at me. I sensed such evil in his smirk and I coward before him. That was the first of many times if I pleasured other men he did not approve of I would be punished.

After the family found out about the abuse I endured from Dean all those years, we were searching in our minds for answers for his deviant behavior. We speculated perhaps Grandma Marsh sexually abused him, or perhaps it was the man she was married to at that time. Dean lived with her off and on from the moment he was born until he turned fifteen. Mom hated her mother and called her the craziest women she had ever known. Over the years I heard her say that time and time again, but she needed her help so she put up with her.

Grandma Marsh had a seemingly strange closeness to Dean so our assumptions of abuse always pointed back towards her. We also considered the possibility he might have been gang raped in Juvey. Whatever the reason, we will never know. I have always felt something dreadful must have happened to him. Not that what might have happened was an excuse to abuse others, but it is unnatural to be as hateful or evil towards other people as he was. I don't believe you're born as a "bad seed." Surely he was taught to be so evil! He wasn't a full-blown misogynist just for the hell of it, or was he? He did seem to take an unusual amount of pleasure from the many girls and women he mentally, physically, and sexually abused over the years.

Dean had a strange and alluring charisma. He was able to entice many people into his snare of lies and deceit. Charles Manson, Ted Bundy, and Jim Jones come to mind when I think of how he could lure people to him. Those who fell into HIS den of iniquity had no idea how he was only using them to get what he wanted. His charm was hypnotic, and he could make people love him whether they wanted to or not.

Dean did not have relationships with people, he only had uses for them. The men he befriended or the women he claimed to love either had something he could take from them for his pleasure or they had a purpose to help him obtain whatever possession he wanted at the time.

When there was nothing left to take from his unsuspecting victims, without explanation or any sense of remorse, he would simply discard them like a used snotty tissue. If you had nothing to offer him, or he couldn't grasp control of you, you were the fortunate one. He would pass you by and your life would be spared.

Dean left me alone for a while. He had a new territory to conquer. He was successful in finding girls closer to his own age, yet still much younger than he was to fulfill his sexual pleasure. He pursued a local girl and charmed the pants right off of her and she became pregnant. She was sixteen and he was seventeen. It was 1964 and abortion as we know it today was not legal, so they were forced to get married. Even if abortion was legal then, it's hard to say if she would have been forced to have one or not. I'm not sure how her parents felt about the issue, but our mother was a firm proponent of abortion, as I would find out years later.

Both the girl and Dean were underage and in order for them to get married her parents and our mother authorized the unwanted nuptials. They were married in April. He turned eighteen in May and she turned seventeen in June. If he had been eighteen when she became pregnant who's to say if the marriage would have even taken place. I know Mom was very proactive in seeing the marriage did transpire. She did not want him to be incarcerated again. Perhaps her parents were not willing to have an unwed daughter giving birth to their grandchild, so they refused to press charges against him. My nephew, my mother's grandson, was born that October. I was eight years old.

The marriage was short lived. Dean kept busy with his new life and his new conquests. Only when he became bored would he return to assert his power over me. Although he left me alone for a brief time, it wasn't long until there were other abusers to take his place.

2

"Man is the only animal whose desires increase as they are fed; the only animal that is never satisfied."

Henry George (1839 – 1897)

I was a couple of months old when my mother divorced my father. My dad loved to drink, a lot, and he became an alcoholic. Mom on the other hand could enjoy a cocktail from time to time without getting totally wasted. She enjoyed going out with friends. They were out with another couple one night and the other woman's husband asked Mom to dance. Mom said he was a fantastic dancer, which really made Dad mad because he knew Mom hated dancing with him. She said Dad was good looking as heck but had no rhythm whatsoever. She said he was about as graceful as a baboon on a high wire. As the night went on Dad proceeded to get drunk and became verbally abusive.

They left the nightclub and as Mom drove home Dad passed out in the back seat. That really made her angry! Not only could he not dance, or would not, but then he got indignant about it, became verbally abusive, and finally passed out in the back seat of the car leaving Mom to drive them home. She was fuming and sick of hearing his drunken snores so she pulled the car to the side of the road. She jumped out of the car and opened the trunk, pulled out the tire iron and, opening the back car door, she started hitting him with it. He woke up screaming, *"What the hell are you doing woman are you crazy?"* He jumped out of the car and she returned to the front seat behind the steering wheel and drove off.

The next day Dad made his way home and asked a neighbor to check and see if the coast was clear before he entered the apartment. He never did raise a hand to Mom and I don't think she ever hit him again. Those evenings out dancing became less frequent. Mom couldn't stand going in public places with him anymore. His drinking became completely out of hand. Returning home after work one night, as many nights before, she found him drunk and passed out on the floor. His breath reeked of whiskey. That was it! She declared "No more!" Mom was tired of being broke because of his drinking and filed for divorce. That was the story she told me for many years. After her death yet another secret would come to life and the real reason she divorced him.

A couple of years after Mom left Dad she met Bob, and they married. That would have been her fourth marriage, or so we thought. For years she never corrected us when we would say she had been married four times. Mom's first marriage she gave birth to my older sister Punkin and my older brother Butch. Her second marriage she gave birth to Dean, her third marriage I was born, and with her fourth husband, Bob, she gave birth to my sister Donna and my brother Karl. My stepfather Bob died when I was in the second grade. I was glad he died! I hated him and I knew being dead meant he wouldn't bother me again. Mom never remarried after Bob died. He was a veteran and as his widow she received monthly benefit payments for the three of us children.

Punkin was married and living elsewhere by then, and Butchy was living on his own and working. Dean was also living elsewhere. Mom, working full time, hired a baby sister for us three younger kids. Those monthly VA benefit payments helped her tremendously. She was able to put a better roof over our heads and keep us fed and clothed much more comfortably than she had in the past. After Bob died I don't think she met a man wealthy enough to marry and gamble away her guaranteed pension. Had she remarried she would have to forfeit those monthly payments. She was in a financial position none of her husbands were ever able to give her and she was enjoying her independence. Determined to remain a widow she was grateful for the benefits and the freedom it brought her.

Mom loved her career as a bookkeeper. One time a male supervisor told her it was too bad she wasn't a man or she would be earning more money. What an asinine remark! She just became a widow making her the breadwinner with three young mouths to feed. So she went in search of other employment and found another bookkeeping job. The owner of the company believed in Mom and gave her the same pay he had been paying the male bookkeeper she was replacing. He was a smart man and knew from the moment he met her he had the most loyal employee he would ever hire. She stayed with the company for over twenty years, and even after her retirement she went back part time to help out.

Before Bob died we would often go and visit his older brother, his wife, and their children. They lived in Missouri and it took a couple of hours to drive to their home. I'm not sure how far away it was but sometimes when we would visit we spent the night in their home. They had a lot of kids. Some were the same age as the three of us and we enjoyed going there. We would play outside all day running around having a great time. My step-aunt prepared plenty of food for us to eat during our stay. She was such a good cook that her husband became extremely obese and could not get out of bed. Making excuses for his condition, he often commented that he injured his back and couldn't work. Mom told us later he was just lazy and didn't want to work. I'm not sure which story was the truth and I really didn't care.

The bedrooms in their house were upstairs so they moved a bed into the family room. He could barely walk, let alone manage the stairs. With the bed downstairs he could watch TV, be close to the kitchen, and rule the house. That bed was his throne. He was a disgusting slob, loud and lazy. With only a sheet over his lap he lounged, perched up on one arm like Jabba the Hutt from *Star Wars*, and barked out his orders. I could tell he was not wearing any underwear, and he never wore a shirt. He always had a beer in one hand and food in the other. His wife would pre-pare whatever he wanted to eat and would dutifully deliver it to him. Her world seemed to revolve around him and I remember watching her fearfully obey his every command. His children feared him too even though he couldn't get out of bed to chase them. He had a beastly effect on his family, and they lived in daily terror under his rule.

One overnight trip to their house was during a summer holiday weekend. The adults spent most of the day and evening drinking and playing cards and all the kids spent the day playing outside. It became late in the evening and everyone was worn out and ready to call it quits. I don't remember how many bedrooms there were, but Mom was given a bed and she put Donna and Karl in bed with her. Bob was given a single size bed to sleep in. I don't know how it came about but it was his suggestion I get into bed with him. I didn't want to sleep with him, but after being scolded to do so I submitted and did as I was told. He pulled the covers over us.

After the lights went out he grabbed my hand and put it down his pants. I pulled away and started crying very loud. It scared me! The truly sad part was, I wasn't scared of what my stepfather was doing to me, I was afraid of how Dean would punish me if he found out. I was terri-fied I would be punished, just as I had been the day I was found in the car with the neighbor boy. I remember how horrible Dean made me feel that day in the car. That night, my sex education, the brainwashing was at work. I felt no love towards my stepfather, nor did he love me, therefore putting my hand down his pants was not supposed to hap-pen. I could never tell anyone what happened to me that night, especially Dean, for fear of being punished.

Mom heard me crying and came into the room to check on me. She asked what was wrong and my stepfather said I must be afraid of the dark. He suggested I go to bed with her and she should put Donna in bed with him. Fine with me, I hated the bastard! How dare he try anything like that with me, I hated being near him. I was too young to think at that moment or even be concerned if he would do the same thing to his own daughter. Only years later did I remember and begin to understand why he never sug-gested putting his son in bed with him. He only requested that us girls be put in bed with him.

Bob would never touch me or anyone else again. Not long after that night he was diagnosed with lung can-cer and died. After my stepfather died our visit's to his brother's home became less frequent, and eventually we stopped going there altogether. I was happy about that. Jabba was disgusting and I hated being around him. Mom couldn't stand the way he treated his wife and children, and she could not understand how my step-aunt devalued her life so much and seemed to worship him. Mom kept in touch with her by phone and would occasionally meet her for lunch. Mom cared for her and felt bad about her situation, but she knew there was nothing she could do to help but offer her friendship.

Shortly after Bob's death we moved again. Mom rented a three-bedroom house. It was smaller than the house we had lived in but it was just Mom, Donna, Karl, and I. It was in a better neighborhood than the previous one. It was cleaner and there was a front and back yard for us to play in. There was a family of six that lived cattycorner across the street from us, and their house had a very steep hill in the back. The husband and wife were younger than Mom, maybe by ten years. They had four children, three daughters and a son. The two youngest girls were close to my age, one two years older, and the youngest was a year younger than me. They became my best friends and they remain my best friends to this day.

After I told my family about my abuse I was curious to know if Donna had been sexually abused. Donna never admitted to any sexual abuse at her father's hands or anyone else. I asked her many times if her father or our brother Dean abused her and she would adamantly say, "*NO, NEVER.*" It was the way she said it that made me concerned for her. She would snap the words out of her mouth, and would immediately change the subject. I understood if anything had happened she would only tell me when she was emotionally able to. I didn't press the issue any more. She was three and a half years younger than me, perhaps too young to remember anything or couldn't bring herself to remember. I could tell she struggled with her own demons for many years. Donna was a proud woman, like Mom and I. She would never admit she had any problems. I believe something cruel did happen to her. She put up a good front for years just as I had: another actress in the making. I would bet my life her own father did something to her that night and, perhaps, other nights.

Donna lived her life much as I did before I received professional counseling. At times she was destructive, self-deprecating, punishing herself. I felt something was ripping her soul apart. She drank heavily, used drugs, and would often call me at work, drunk, blaming me for all of her problems. Many things tormented her. I know she was jealous of the attention Dean paid to me all those years. Donna hated that he pushed her aside and took me alone on trips with him in his car or on his motorcycle. He never took her or Karl on trips or gave them presents or money. He was cruel to them and, sadly, in different ways, Dean and I both shoved it in their faces that I was his favorite. I was a spoiled brat at times, but flaunting being his favorite sometimes made me feel better about what he was doing to me. I was hurting so I had to hurt them too.

When Dean wasn't sexually abusing me he was psychologically tormenting me, Donna, and Karl. He would make remarks such as, *"You're so pretty but you're so dumb,"* and end his remarks with his trademark sinister smirk. He would call us stupid little kids and was relentless with other disparaging remarks, which slowly chipped away at our self-esteem. He was such a bastard. If he saw us laughing and having fun he would have to intervene with some wicked remark to spoil our moment. His soul was so plagued full of hatred for life he couldn't stand to see others enjoying it. He had to be in control of every moment. He had to be the Puppet Master pulling the strings. If we did laugh and have fun it was only because he permitted it. Whatever he wanted the situation to be, it would be. We always walked on eggshells around him.

I know Mom saw how Dean treated us and she would tell him to leave us alone. Her scolding him made him even more determined to obliterate our moments of happiness. It was pure evil bursting out of him, like lava spewing from a volcano there was just no stopping it. He was a ravenous beast, and he loved to torture us. It fed his ego and I could tell he received absolute pleasure from it. Once he realized just how much mental anguish he could pile upon us the crueler he became. Whenever he saw a moment of complete goodness or innocence he had to destroy it.

Karl told me how Dean used to bully him, relentlessly. Karl went to live with Dean in California after he graduated from high school, and they worked together as construction laborers. One day Dean started with the belittling remarks until Karl couldn't take it anymore. He stood up to him and told him to back off or he would kick his ass. He said that was the first time he ever saw a look of shock on Dean's face. Karl had startled him with his statement. Slowly a slight smirk came to Dean's face and he went over and put his arm around Karl and patted him on the back. He was taking credit for bringing Karl into manhood. Once again it was about him, and he could not let anyone get one over on him. I'm not sure if Mom ever saw the absolute evilness in Dean or she just didn't want to see it. She was in complete denial. Years later she was unwillingly driven to come to terms with Dean's wickedness and she would have no choice but to accept the fact she had spawned such evil.

After I revealed the years of incest, Donna realized she never had any reason to be jealous of me. She began to feel bad that she had such hateful, jealous, feelings towards me all those years. Sharing our stories of what Dean did to us through the years was healing for both of us. We finally came to understand it was Dean who had destroyed our sisterly bond. Donna and I struggled for years to repair our relationship. Some sibling rivalry is only natural I think. However, thanks to him we struggled with a much deeper contention for each other.

My sister would never know how jealous I was of her in later years. She had something I would never have, two beautiful children. Donna was a good person, but she struggled with motherhood. She did the best she could. Unfortunately, Mom's nurturing gave little to be desired, therefore not much of a role model for us. Donna had a big heart and didn't give a damn what people thought of her. I wish I could have been more like her. Sadly my little sister died of breast cancer at the age of forty-six. By her side watching her pass away, I prayed for her spirit to be free of pain and be at peace. It was hard for me to show her any love. I hope she knows now how much I do love her.

3

Not long after my parents divorced Dad's mother, Grandma Groom, moved in with him. Grandpa Groom died a few years earlier and she was more than willing to move in with Dad. It gave her a new purpose, and she could once again take care of her son. She was only five foot tall and Dad called her Shorty. Grandma gave birth to thirteen children and Dad was her baby boy. She made no bones about the fact he was her favorite living child and in her eyes he could do no wrong. During the Spanish Flu Pandemic of 1918-1919 she lost several of her babies and some of them were boys. Dad was her only living son and Grandma adored him.

Grandma married Grandpa Groom in 1911 when she was fifteen and he was twenty-six. It wasn't uncommon during those times for older men to marry much younger girls. Her family didn't mind her marrying an older man because there were twelve other children and it would be one less mouth to feed. Her parents wanted the girls to marry, but they needed to keep the boys single and at home working the farm. Of course, today an older man marring a fifteen-year-old girl might be considered statutory rape.

When I turned twenty-five, still single, never married, Grandma Groom called me an old maid. Her statement hurt my feelings but I tried to understand her generation's attitude. Most women from her era were married at a young age. I was forty-one when I married. Had she been alive it would have upset her that I waited so long, but I'm sure she would have been happy that it finally happened. Grandma had no clue what it was like to be a single independent woman. She spent her life being a devoted housewife and mother, and thought I should do the same. I really loved Grandma Groom. She was sweet, affectionate, and very loving towards me. I only met my other grandmother, Grandma Marsh, maybe once or twice and I didn't like her at all. She was a big nasty loud-mouthed old woman and I could tell she didn't care for me one bit. Dean was her favorite.

Dad rented a two-bedroom apartment in Missouri for him and Grandma Groom. It was in a big brick building. The bricks were not a pretty red color, but a dirty ugly

beige. From the sidewalk you would climb a set of concrete stairs to get to the front door. Going through the
main glass door their apartment was the first door on the
left, and it overlooked the sidewalk and street. I would sit
at the front window watching and waiting for Dad to come
home from work.

Grandma Groom was French, born in Canada, and she
thoroughly enjoyed cooking for Dad and me. Her specialty
was cream puff pastries. She made the pastries and the
vanilla filling from scratch and it was always a special treat.
She was a great cook, and fed Dad and I very well. In the
summers she wore lightweight housedresses, like moo
moos but shorter. I believe they call them patio dresses
today. I loved visiting them. There were some happy times,
innocent times. I could just be a little girl and be spoiled.

Mom told me Dad never paid one cent of child support. He told her he knew she would go hungry before
she let any of her children go without food. He didn't care
if she had anything to eat or not. After my stepfather Bob
died, I spent a lot of summers with Grandma and Dad. Even
though he never helped Mom by giving her any money, it
was a financial relief for her that I stayed with them whenever possible, and she knew I would be fed well. Dad never
gave Mom any money to buy items that I might need, but
he often bought gifts for me.

Dad worked for a school-supply company and during
the school year I would occasionally receive a box contain-
ing toys and clothes from him. The boxes would be deliv-
ered in a truck along with other supplies the elementary

school had ordered. Once it arrived, the principal's office secretaries would call over the intercom to my classroom and have the teacher send me up to the office to receive my gift-box. The office secretary's thought sending me gifts was the sweetest thing. They would say, "*You have such a wonderful thoughtful father.*" A few years later I would be sent to the principal's office many times but it wasn't to pick up gifts.

The summers I spent with Dad and Grandma, Monday through Friday starting at five o'clock, I would sit at the front apartment window with blissful anticipation, waiting for him to come home from work. Like an excited puppy in the window fidgeting, I would start jumping around with joy as soon as I saw him turn the corner of the building. He only lived a block or two from the school-supply company where he worked so he didn't need to buy a car. Perhaps he could not afford to buy one, which was more likely. One night Dad was late coming home from work. Finally, Grandma and I ate dinner without him, but as soon as I was finished eating I was back at the window watching and waiting.

After a while a yellow cab pulled up in front of the apartment building. The cab driver got out to open the back door. I told Grandma about the cab pulling up and she joined me at the window. The driver was a black man with a nice smile wearing a uniform and a cap. He was quite small in stature compared to Dad, who was a slender man but stood six foot two. He opened the back door and stood there holding it open. It was dark and I couldn't see in the back seat. After several minutes the driver reached in the back seat of the cab to help the passenger out. He hoisted the man's arm over his shoulder and reached around his side to help him walk up the stairs. Not until then did I realize it was Dad. I thought, "Poor little black man." Dad completely covered him like a shroud.

Grandma flew out the door and down the stairs to help the driver, but he insisted he could get Dad inside by himself. He suggested she could hold the doors open for him. I was crying by then and yelling, *"Daddy's been hurt,"* and this sweet man with the nice smile tried to assure me he was ok, he wasn't hurt. He finally got Dad up the stairs and into his bedroom where he gently laid him on the bed. Grandma was frantically pacing back and forth, and her hands were clasped as if she were praying. She thanked the driver over and over. After he got Dad into bed she went to get her money to pay him. As I looked up at the cab driver I could see he was an older man whose face was weathered and worn. He had a very gentle way about him and I felt safe in his presence. He wiped a tear off my face and in his broken Southern English said, *"Don't chew worry little gal yo daddy's goanna be ok, by morn-in you jis wait and see he's goanna be ok."*

I went and stood by Dad's bed and looked at his face to make sure he was ok and quickly turned away. The smell almost made me vomit. He smelled as if he'd bathed and washed his clothes in whiskey, and he was snoring loudly. He was out cold. I was getting angry and immediately stopped crying. I don't remember exactly how old I was, maybe seven or eight, possibly younger, but I knew drinking lots of whiskey was bad. I knew because Mom would talk about his drinking all the time. She never elaborated, but she made me aware his drinking made him do things he normally wouldn't do if he were sober. It wasn't until after Dad died and I was much older did she ever talk badly about him. I always admired her for not talking trash about him in front of me as a child.

I was smart enough to know that when he drank whisky he went from the daddy I loved to the cantankerous old bastard I hated to be around. Dad kept his whiskey bottle proudly sitting on his bedroom dresser. After the cab driver left I grabbed his whisky bottle and ran to the bathroom, which was located right across from his room. I started pouring the whiskey down the sink and Grandma ran in yelling at me to stop. Her yelling woke him up and he jumped out of bed. Half the bottle was down the sink before he grabbed it out of my hand. He was angry but so drunk he could hardly walk. Grandma went back to the living room to watch TV.

Dad grabbed me and took me to his room. Whenever I got in trouble he would throw me over his knees and pretend to spank me. He did the same that night as he did a hundred times before and I just laid there waiting for the imaginary spanking to end. This time was different, something was happening. I became frightened but I didn't move. His hand went from pretending to spank me, went down inside the back of my pants, and he started fondling me. I'm not sure why I didn't pull away. I was confused, and was not sure what I should do, so I just laid there waiting for it to stop.

Scared and confused, I lay there thinking I did something really bad this time and this was my punishment. Thinking back I wondered why he could never bring himself to spank me but he could do unspeakable things to me. I would have preferred to be strung between two posts and beaten on my bare back with a leather whip than suffer this kind of punishment. I sensed my inner light diminishing a little more, as if my candle were running out of wick and becoming weaker and weaker. My essence, just like my body, was limp and becoming more lifeless.

The fondling seemed to go on forever. Finally, he stopped, lifted me off his lap and pushed me away. He grumbled something nasty and fell back on the bed and started snoring again. I no longer looked at him as my daddy. From that moment on he was just Dad. I didn't feel the love for him like I did before. I felt scared and dazed. I ran to the living room and sat next to Grandma to feel safe. I learned my lesson. I never touched his whiskey bottle again. The blissful nights of waiting in the window for my daddy ceased that night.

Shortly after Mom passed away my older sister, Punkin, shared a secret with me. When she was sixteen Dad got drunk and fondled her. Punkin told Mom what he did to her and that was the real reason they divorced. Mom never told me that story. I think she was ashamed she had married someone who could do something so dreadful. Punkin was not Dad's biological daughter so I'm sure it never crossed Mom's mind his drinking would lead him to do the same thing to me. If she thought he would commit such a horrible act with his own daughter Mom would never have let me visit him.

The next morning Dad walked into the kitchen. Grandma and I were already up eating breakfast. I sheepishly looked up at him. Even as young as I was I could tell he had no clue how he got home the night before. I started telling him about the sweet old man, the black cab driver, who brought him home and helped put him in bed. Dad became enraged as the story went on. He blurted out indignantly, *"I don't need anybody's help to get in bed let alone help from a n____r."* I hate that word! Mom made me aware the N word carried a bad connotation. I hate hearing it or saying it, so I refuse to type it. Dad's remark confused me and it took years to understand how he developed such hatred for black people.

Not long after that night I joined a softball league. I was a tomboy: very competitive, a good athlete, and I excelled at softball. On another visit to Dad and Grandma's, after I arrived, walking past his room something caught my eye. It stopped me dead in my tracks. Unafraid, I ran into his room and grabbed it. It was a beautiful new baseball bat and, of course, I thought it was a gift for me. I was happy and wearing the biggest smile. I picked it up and began to turn to thank him. I didn't get completely turned around when he reached over me and took it from my hands. He placed it back on the floor, leaning it against the headboard. He was not callous or forceful taking it away from me, and

I think he felt bad because he had no gifts to give me, but he didn't want me to get attached to it either. It was his and he was not about to give up possession of his weapon. He said it was his n_____r knocker. I was upset it wasn't a gift for me and I could not comprehend it being used as a weapon. Remembering the little old black man who was so sweet and kind, how could Dad want to hurt someone who was so nice to us, to him? I remember thinking, *"My dad is the bad man, not the black man."* My immature brain couldn't handle the hurt or the hate. There was no logic to any of it.

Shortly after the incident of the baseball bat a black girl came to my grade school. I went to an all white school, and it surprised me when she timidly walked into my classroom. She was shy, sweet and scared but something drew me to her and I liked her immediately, and wanted to befriend her. I could tell she was glad to have a friend. Her name was Charmaine, and the kids would tease her and call her toilet paper. I felt sad for her. I always stand up for the underdog, perhaps because I've felt that way myself from time to time.

The kids became relentless with their taunting. Day after day their heckling became more malicious. *"Toilet paper, toilet paper."* Then they turned on me and started calling me *"n_____r lover."* Over and over, *"n_____r lover, n_____r lover."* I was confused. I knew their words carried a severe accusation, but I kept thinking I am not a bad person. I wanted to be her friend, but the more hateful my white friends became towards me the more afraid I became. I felt torn and alone in my quest to befriend her, and I started to withdraw from her. Not completely avoiding her, but I wasn't as obvious about our friendship as before. I wasn't strong enough to continue our relationship as it was. I know she sensed my weakness and probably felt I let her down. I watched in sorrow her growing sadness. I always felt bad for not being stronger and letting others influence my friendship with her. My self-esteem was not strong enough, I was just a child, and it was a tough lesson. Now, as an adult and stronger I will never allow anyone to tell me who to befriend, love, or stand up for, ever again.

Mom knew what a bigot Dad was and always tried to counter balance his beliefs by telling me just because people were black did not make them bad. However, her actions would confuse me. When we drove through the black section of town she would tell us to lock the doors. As a child I had not been around many black people, but the ones I had were always nice to me. The only bad people I knew were white. They were not only sexually abusing me, but emotionally they were trying to infect me with their racist sickness. One day I went back to school and Charmaine was gone. I never saw her again and I was very saddened by that.

A few years later mom told me that Grandpa Groom had been in the KKK, and Dad had served a brief stint with the Klan. It all began to make sense, all those nasty remarks through the years about black people. Such hatred for one race went from generation to generation and my mother wanted to make damn sure Dad's ignorant beliefs were not passed on to me.

Dad and Grandma moved to Texas in 1970, and I celebrated my fourteenth birthday in March that year. The three of us corresponded by phone and mail during my Junior and Senior High School years. I missed Dad but not as much as I missed Grandma Groom. I didn't see them again until after my High School graduation in 1974, the same year Dad and Grandma had relocated to Arkansas. After I finished High School I would visit them several times a year for a long weekend visit. The drive from Kansas City was an eight-hour trip and I could miss one day of work but not two. I would leave on a Friday morning and return to Kansas City the following Sunday evening.

It wasn't long after graduation Dad was diagnosed with Lung cancer. When the disease overcame him and Grandma was not able to care for him anymore, he was admitted to the VA Hospital in Little Rock. It was about two hours farther south from Grandmas, and I would stop and spend the night with her, both to and from the hospital. One visit Dad mentioned if I came to see him and he was in the *"other wing"* it meant he was a goner. He lifted his arm from the bed, I looked in the direction he was pointing with his finger, and he said, *"That's where they put us old vet's who don't have much time left."* I thought he had more time.

Due to him being in the hospital, I didn't wait as long between visits to make the long drive again. That trip, I went to his original room and was told they moved him to the other wing. Slowly, and with great uncertainty, I walked towards the double doors. Frozen by fear, I stood at the doorway, staring and listening in disbelief. It was a large room and it seemed as big as a football field. There were rows upon rows of beds with white sheets, and underneath the sheets lay dying men. Some looked as if they were already dead. Not one bed was empty. Walking rapidly past each deathbed going in the direction of his, I was shocked to see their corpselike faces. I tried to keep my eyes diverted to the floor, but I could not avoid the sounds that echoed throughout the room piercing my ears. The groans of death made me cringe as if I was hearing the shrieking sounds of fingernails scratching across a chalkboard.

I tried not to show my anguish, but when Dad looked up at my face my distress was obvious. I bent down to kiss his cheek and hug him. His hand flew up to his face to refuse my gesture. *"NO"* he barked. He didn't want me to touch him. He said, *"I don't want to infect you."* His ignorance towards cancer was similar to the attitude of many people around the world towards AIDS when it first became known. By touching him he thought he would pollute me with his cancer. What he didn't realize was, by touching me the way he did many years ago I was already infected. I was plague-ridden with a cancer not from his blood, but from his horrific actions and it exacerbated in my soul. Less than a month after my visit he died. It was 1978, and he was only fifty-eight.

4

> *"Choose rather to be strong of soul than strong of body."*
>
> **Pythagoras** (570 BC – 490 BC)

For a short time I was left alone by my various abusers to be a child with no worries in the world. My step Dad was dead, and when I went to visit Grandma and Dad I knew staying close to Grandma would keep him away from me. Fortunately for me, at least, Dean was busy with his life devouring the souls of other unwilling victims who were getting snared into his den of indulgence.

What an intriguing concept: left alone to be a child, to laugh, to play, to cry. Crying, not because I was being forced into a sexual situation but because I was learning right from wrong on my own accord. I was exploring life, as a child should: investigating, diving into each new day with no fear, stumbling and picking myself up. I was learning life's lessons, and for a brief moment in time I was able to walk down my own pathway of life.

Due to the incensed rage boiling inside me, for the longest time I thought there were no childhood memories worth holding on to. But once the fog of anguish lifted I could look back at my life and search for a few happy moments. There were a few. They started the day we moved across the street from the house with the big steep hill. We moved during the summer, and the following fall I would attend a new school, starting in the second grade. It was one of the best days of my life. I spotted someone playing in the yard with the steep hill. With blonde hair and big brown eyes, her laugh was infectious and I ran over to meet her. She was full of life. Her inner light radiated brightly and I knew I wanted to be her friend. The moment Dora and I met we were inseparable. She and her middle sister would become my best friends for life.

Their house with the steep hill was a perfect place for snow sledding. At the bottom of the hill it opened into a large flat field with plenty of room to slow down before crashing into the fence. One year Butchy bought me a pair of toy wooden skis. I would strap them on and ski down the hill. The first couple of times I skied down, Butchy and Dean walked down the hill and picked me up under each arm and walked back up the hill with my feet and skis dangling, as if I was riding a ski lift. They became exhausted after two or three times and gave up, so I had to take them off and walk up the hill myself.

I loved living across the street from Dora. Happily glued at the hip, we were together day and night. I would spend the night at her house or she would be at mine. If you saw one of us the other was most certainly close by. Dora had a dirt bike and we would ride it all the time exploring the neighborhood together. We were tomboys. We liked dolls but we preferred to be outside wrestling or playing baseball with the boys. During the winters we built snow huts and snowmen in their big field. Ours were always better built than the boys. We enjoyed competing against the boys in the neighborhood.

Dean acquired a new passion, and became involved with racing cars and riding motorcycles. He purchased a mini bike and a go-cart for me and brought them to Mom's house. Dora and I drove each one pushing them to their limits up and down the street, dodging parked cars, swerving, trying not to crash. We were fearless. Like *Evel Knievel.* I loved competing and outperforming everyone, especially the boys. I'm not sure what Dora's motive was, maybe it was to keep up with me. But I felt I must outperform everyone, the girls and the boys. Driven by some unforeseen force, I felt compelled to excel in whatever I immersed myself into. My competitiveness would come into play throughout my whole life, personally and professionally.

Dean would look at me and smirk, always calling me stupid, so I suppose that was my way of proving my self-worth. If I couldn't prove it with my mind I would do it with my body through sports. Little did I know the lessons I was learning were teaching me how to use my body years later to prove my worthiness, but it wasn't through sports. As a child some lessons are learned inadvertently. The verbal, emotional and sexual abuse I received from Dean was, unknowingly, also teaching me how to emasculate the males who happened to cross my path.

I was not conscience of it, but over the years I picked up a few of Dean's bad traits and became quite a bitch criticizing and belittling men, both their good qualities and their bad. I loved men, lots of them over the years, but tearing them down made me feel better about myself. Like breathing, cruelly badgering men came natural to me. There was no special effort. I'm sure my husband would say it is something I still struggle with today. Every day I make a conscience effort not to be disparaging towards him or other men.

At one point, before I cried out for help, I became incensed and carried a deep hatred for men. A few of my friends nicknamed me *"The Man Eater."* I was completely filled with vicious anger towards men, not with anyone in particular but all of them. I could not understand why I felt the way I did. All I knew was that I hated every single man in the world and if they all dropped dead I would not have given a damn. At times I could be such a bitch, and I would make it my mission to verbally render impotent any man who strayed my way. I have heard it said the male ego can be fragile, and with the strike of a spoken word I could snap a man's ego right in half.

My hunger to destroy any man who happened to cross my path became insatiable. I became completely possessed.

For the sins of a few, I felt I must punish the whole male species. During one therapy session I had a very profound epiphany: all my life I punished both the men who tried to love me, and the men who would not love me. I realized I was chastising all of them for my flawed deficiency, not theirs. It was a harsh realization to deal with but all along it was I, not them, who was incapable of being loved or loving. I didn't know how to love them or myself.

I had fleeting moments of happiness being a child and being left alone sexually. Sadly there were times when I became confused and wondered why I was left alone, untouched. During those moments I felt unloved, unwanted, rejected. My sexual abuse taught me that in order to be loved by a man I must give them sex, otherwise they wouldn't love me. Yes there were men who truly loved me along the way, but there were many that pretended to love me or like me just to get laid.

Not long after we moved across from Dora's house Butchy came back home to live with us. He was working at night and he would sleep during the day. One day I was running and playing around the house, being very noisy. After a while he woke up from the noisy laughter. He asked me to come to his room and get in bed with him. Alarmed by his request, I stopped laughing but I complied.

Crawling under the covers I could tell he only had under-wear on. He was lying on his side and he put my back to his chest. Eyes wide open, laying there, tense, waiting and waiting. I was not sleepy and I couldn't fall asleep. I'm not sure know how long I waited for him to touch me or make me touch him. It seemed forever but nothing happened, nothing at all. A few moments went by and, softly snoring, he was sleeping once again. I became confused and discouraged. I carefully got out of bed and went into the other room. I was thinking Butchy doesn't love me because he didn't do anything sexual to me. I sat in a chair with my arms folded, my head hung low, and a puffed out bottom lip. I was sulking for being rejected by him. Why didn't he touch me, doesn't he love me? I became sad, mad, and most definitely confused.

After that confusing moment I felt the special bond we previously had was forever severed. Butchy didn't love me the way Dean did, and for years I didn't feel as close to him as I did with Dean. I thought Dean was the only one who truly loved me.

Years later I came to understand how healthy our relationship really was. Butchy was exhausted that day and all he wanted to do was to calm me down and cuddle so he could get some sleep. He worked at night and needed to sleep during the day. Now I understand the pure sweetness of the moment. A child should be able to lovingly cuddle with an adult without lying in terror of what might happen to them. That is how a relationship between an adult and a child should be. Softly cuddling with men was foreign to me. Every other time I was in bed with an adult male a sexual encounter was forced upon me.

It took many years to finally comprehend I had more to offer men than just sex. A few months after I started therapy I shared with Butchy how that encounter made me feel.

Together I told Butchy and Karl I didn't think they loved me through the years because they never tried anything sexual with me. It utterly broke my heart to witness how my feelings towards them over the years wounded them. Never before had I seen grown men fall to their knees, burst into tears, and cry out loud with no dishonor whatsoever. They were in agony over what I had just shared with them and absolutely grief-stricken for me. They had no idea the pain and suffering I went through all those years. We cried, we hugged, and we grieved the remainder of the day for that lost little girl. We started reclaiming our relationships and are extremely close now. I love them both dearly and I am grateful and happy they love me the way brothers should love their sister. They are both gentlemen, wonderful husbands and fathers, and it is marvelous to see the healthy relationships they have with their families.

Over the years I would lay with men but I could not let them cuddle with me. I could not lay with my back to a man without having a panic attack. Whether I was clothed or not, it didn't matter. Before I entered therapy my nephew Roy came to visit me in Florida. He was Donna's first born and I loved him as if he were my own. When he was just a few months old I threatened my sister by telling her I would take her to court and take him away from her. She was spiraling out of control, drinking, doing drugs, partying all night, and I believed she had no business having a child. Who was I to judge? I never did take her to court. I knew deep down I would not have been any better at being a parent because I was just as out of control, if not more so.

They were just idle threats and they didn't stop her. We both continued on our own descent into the darkness of self-abuse.

Roy was ten or eleven when he came to visit. I was excited to see him. It was during his summer vacation and I planned a lot of activities for us. I lived in a one-bedroom apartment and made a bed for him on the couch. The first night he was there he got up off the couch and crawled into bed with me. He came up behind me, wrapped his arms around me, and snuggled me. He told me how much he loved me and how happy he was to visit with me and asked if he could sleep with me.

I froze from anxiety and, starting to panic, I felt sick to my stomach. I wanted to jerk away from him, but I was afraid I might scare him. I didn't understand what was happening to me. I felt like I was going to crawl right out of my skin and I began to hyperventilate. Trying to remain calm, careful not to alarm him, I told him how happy I was he came to visit me.

As soon as I knew he was asleep I got up and went to the couch. My muscles ached from being so tense. I fixed myself a drink and lit a cigarette. I felt like I was going to throw up. I was getting mad at myself and thinking what in the hell is going on, what is wrong with me why did I panic? I knew it was just an innocent, loving, gesture and all he wanted was to hug me but I couldn't.

Years after therapy, living with my husband, the man I trust the most, I have the same panic attacks when he tries to cuddle up to my back. My body becomes tense and my muscles ache. Trying to disguise my anxiety, I make him turn over so I can lay with his back to me. Going through menopause was convenient because I would use the excuse that I was too hot to be so close to him. I felt bad and knew his feelings were hurt and he felt rejected time and time again. His attempts to hug me completely frightened me, and I had no idea why I would panic. Our first years of marriage I could not share with him the shear pain and terror I felt when he tried to snuggle up to me. I remembered how I felt when my nephew tried to cuddle with me and it was the same.

Being touched in any manner has always been difficult for me. Someone trying to hold my hand or innocently touch my arm, the anxiety overwhelms me and I must pull away. Getting ready for my wedding day, a dear friend of mine owned a nail salon and offered to give me a manicure and pedicure as a gift for my special day. I told her no thank you, but she kept insisting. Someone offered me a Xanex to help calm my nerves, but even with that it was difficult to sit still and keep from throwing up. Thankfully, without any drugs I am now able to sit through a pedicure without panicking, but I still cannot let them touch or massage my legs. I remember when my niece came to visit me in Florida. As a professional massage therapist she offered to give me a massage. I informed her I had never been able to let anyone give me a massage, and just the thought of one makes me panic. She started touching the back of my neck. Immediately I starting shaking and, breaking out in a sweat, I jumped off the table and could not let her continue.

Not long ago, I purchased and read a book by E. Sue Blume titled, <u>Secret Survivors: Uncovering Incest and Its Aftereffects in Women</u> (Ballantine, 1991). Her book has helped me tremendously and the following are a few excerpts that helped me understand my panic attacks. She says, *"My book unveils a consistent pattern of emotional and behavioral aftereffects, evidence that incest has more complex and far-reaching consequences than other works have recognized. I call this pattern Post-Incest Syndrome."* (Preface P-xiv)

She continues to say, *"She is frightened or enraged when someone touches her by surprise, or when someone hugs her without asking, or when someone playfully grabs her from behind. She is overwhelmed when her movement is contained or she is trapped. Her gut reaction may be to snap at you or even punch you if you do this, or she may become paralyzed and terrorized."* (P-46)

Finally, Blume says that, *"Touch can be frightening, angering, or painful to an incest survivor. She frequently misinterprets it."* (P-193)

After reading these sections in the book I thought to myself, "I'm not crazy after all. There is a reason why I feel this way." Feeling jubilant, letting out a sigh of relief, I began to understand why I experienced the panic attacks. Not waiting another moment, I called my husband to find out exactly what time he would be home from work. Before he was half way through the door I started sharing what I had read. I was talking so fast he was confused but he could see my excitement and let me keep talking. I was finally able to share with him what I had been going through the first ten years of our marriage. All those years I was afraid to tell him about the pain I would experience when he tried to touch me or hug me from behind. I didn't understand why I was experiencing those feelings, therefore how could I possibly explain it to him at the time. Those feelings frightened me, and perhaps I was afraid he would think I was crazy too.

I know over the years he felt rejected time and time again. Now both of us were beginning to understand I was not refusing him, I was trying to reject the incapacitating fear I felt during those times. Having completed therapy, I thought I was healed. I acted as though I were. I felt I had to. I didn't want any residual effects from the incest. I wanted to be done with it. My husband was right, another revelation. The things I continue to read in <u>Secret Survivors</u> (Ballantine, 1991) are helping me to understand there are aftereffects of the abuse I may never over come but I can learn to deal with them when they surface and be in control of them, instead of them controlling me.

Ms. Blume also writes about Posttraumatic Stress Disorder in her book and I was curious to read more on the subject. I am not diagnosing myself but perhaps what I have experienced is a symptom I developed, not only from the sexual abuse as a child but the rape I endured as an adult. I found an in-depth definition of this disorder in many sources via the Internet and the local Library.

The common definition I found in these sources is similar to this shortened version, *"Posttraumatic Stress Disorder is the development of symptoms following exposure to an extreme traumatic stress or involving direct personal experience of an event that involves actual or threatened death or serious injury, or other threat to one's integrity."*

Also commonly used in the definition is, *"Traumatic events include, but are not limited to military combat, violent personal assault (sexual assault, physical attack, robbery, mugging), being kidnapped, being taken hostage, terrorist attack, torture. For children, sexually traumatic events may include developmentally inappropriate sexual experiences without threatened or actual violence or injury."*

Ms. Blume argues in her book <u>Secret Survivors</u> (Ballantine, 1991) that incest is a form of torture and should also be listed in the definition. I concur!

5

> *"The devil hath power to assume a pleasing shape."*
> **William Shakespeare** (1564 - 1616) *"Hamlet"*

Dora and I were very active and preferred to be outside roughhousing or playing some sport with the boys. One day while playing baseball with the neighborhood kids I ran home to use the bathroom. I was in a hurry because I wanted to get back outside to play. I looked down and the toilet was full of blood. I was furious and screamed out loud, *"Damn it."* I was twelve years old and I knew what was happening and I didn't like it one bit. Mom told me when she started her period she cried with such fear because she thought she was dying of cancer. Her mother never told her anything about her body and the changes it would go through. The nurse at school had the unpleasant duty of telling Mom why a woman has a monthly period and all of the other not so pleasurable stuff that comes with it. Mom said the conversation she had with the nurse was cold and unsympathetic and she wanted to spare my sisters and I from having such a traumatic experience. She gave us just enough information to keep us from being shocked when that moment came but she never continued the discussions much further. I don't think Mom and I really ever had "The Talk."

Mom thought of herself as a modern woman but it was obvious having such intimate conversations with my sisters and I was excruciatingly uncomfortable for her. On the other hand if you wanted to talk politics or world affairs she could debate with the best of them and continue talking all day. For her to initiate any kind of intimate conversation was difficult, but if we asked her a question she would answer it the best she could. Consequently, I believed starting my period meant I would have to give up being a tomboy and of course it meant growing up. I hated the thought of growing up. I chuckle about it now, but seeing the blood that first time I sat there crying and saying over and over, "*I don't want to grow up.*" I wanted to stay in my childhood. I was not ready to move into that phase of becoming a woman. I was having fun being a child and the thought of growing up disgusted me.

I thought growing up meant being prissy, wearing dresses, being a girly girl. I was starting a new chapter in my life and I wanted no part of it. My body was changing and how boys looked at me started changing too.

Slowly I began to embrace how the boys were starting to notice me. But unfortunately, as my body changed, it altered how my brother Dean looked at me as well.

Occasionally Mom would give us kids little pep talks and her favorite saying came from Shakespeare. In her shortened version she would say, *"To thy own self be true. You can be whatever you want to be."* I approached her with my dilemma about growing up and the confusion of thinking I had to act prissy now because I started my period. I told her I wanted to continue being a tomboy. Mom assured me I could embrace being a woman and still enjoy participating in sports. She said it was ok, I could be whatever I wanted to be, and I could do whatever I wanted to do. She firmly conveyed that being a woman and having a period was not a handicap.

Mom was happy to see the world was changing for women and she wanted her daughters to take advantage of every opportunity. She wanted us to enter into whatever activity we were interested in, within reason of course, ethically and financially. Her new employer treated her with dignity and respect and she was becoming more confident. She became involved in various women's groups and it made her feel good she could finally lead by example. She could talk the talk, now she was walking the walk. She hoped in our lifetime we would not be told, *"Too bad you're not a man or you could earn more money."* We're getting somewhat closer to equality in the workplace. It is not said aloud to our face but our salaries still reflect that antiquated way of thinking.

Dean had remarried, and they moved to New Mexico. He wasn't around to tear me down emotionally or abuse me sexually anymore. I was free from his disapproval and I began accepting this new phase of my life. Mom's strength and confidence was contagious and I wanted to be like her. Imitating her I began wearing makeup and dressing up. It felt good to dress up, and it made me feel pretty. My self-confidence was growing, and I even tried out for cheerleading during Junior High. Not able to secure a spot on the cheerleading squad, I then tried out for a position on the drill team and was accepted. I was elected co-captain of the team along with a friend of mine. Sprouting my wings, I felt strong and more secure with myself. With growing confidence and becoming more sociable I was voted first runner up for School Queen during eighth grade. Mom was right, I could be whatever I wanted to be and I had choices.

Mom loved being an independent working woman. Had she remarried I seriously doubt she would have stayed home and conceded to being a housewife. She hated housework. The house was kept fairly clean but extremely cluttered. Being older than Donna and Karl, I unwittingly became Mom's housekeeper and cook. The cooking part I liked, but I hated cleaning house. Mom taught me how to bake desserts, make chicken and homemade noodles, and I can make a tasty pot roast too.

Most days I tried to have dinner ready for Mom when she came home from work. Other days it was pretty simple and quick to open a box of macaroni and cheese and throw it on the stove. Donna, Karl and I thought it was the best meal in the world and we would eat right out of the pan. When we were younger, before Mom received the VA benefits and working at her new job, a box of mac and cheese was all she could afford. We would eagerly watch her prepare a box of mac and cheese, and when it was done she would sit silently and watch us devour it. Mom would go without a single bite to make sure her children had enough to eat. There were many days I know she went hungry but never complained.

With Mom working and the three of us left to our own devices, many days I thought because I was older I should be in charge and responsible for Donna and Karl. The power went to my head, and it gave me some affirmation to my self-worthiness. Bossing the two of them around they continually rebelled against my orders to do any house chores. I was their sister, their equal, not their mother or guardian. I took the role literally, and played the part of housewife and mother while Mom was at work. I'm not sure by doing so it might have played a big part in not wanting to have children. It seemed I had already fulfilled the role of mother by taking care of my younger brother and sister. Perhaps other secrets later in my life played a big part in not wanting to have children as well.

For years I had this voracious drive to be in control of everyone and every situation. Years later, my family nicknamed me "The General" because I bossed everyone around. Returning home for the Holidays I would spout out the orders I thought everyone should perform to help prepare for whatever event was coming up. I acted as the matriarch, the hostess. Mom really didn't mind that I took some control of organizing the events. She was happy to have all of us together but she was not into entertaining or preparing for any family events. Neither my family nor I could understand my obsession to have everything perfect. I know it used to really irritate the family my issuing orders, acting as if I was in charge of everyone.

I finally came to understand my obsession of wanting to control the universe; the absolute need for perfection. I couldn't control the abuse so I tried desperately to control the world around me. It was mania running through my veins. I needed total perfection in everything I did and needed control of those around me. Since counseling, I am getting better at letting go of trying to control everything. At times it is still a struggle, but I am learning how to lead without being bossy. I am also learning how to allow others to offer and participate however they choose to help in planning any event. I can't do it all, and I now know its ok to accept and let others do their part and not worry about absolute perfection. Trying to achieve perfection can be an impossible task and the stress of trying to attain it is exhausting. I'm not perfect and I cannot make others perform perfectly. Now able to relax, somewhat, and just let things happen as they may.

Again, not diagnosing myself but I do believe that I developed mild to moderate obsessive/compulsive tendencies. What Dean and the others did to me kept absolute control over me. I had to try and control something, anything, and everything, and because of that I was christened: "The General."

In March of 1969 I turned thirteen. I was doing well in school, and I had a lot of friends. Life was innocently unfolding before me and I was happy. Becoming more self-confident, I was enjoying my time with the drill team and being nominated for School Queen certainly helped boost my self-esteem. I was having fun, and on my way to becoming the women I was supposed to be. Watching Mom become more confident I wanted to emulate her and I was taking greater pride in my clothing, hair and makeup. I was happy and my world was full of light and promise. The world seemed colorful and alive, with billions of wonderful possibilities. Shortly after my thirteenth birthday, in the blink of an eye, the innocence of childhood I had begun to recapture would be ripped from me forever.

Most spring days are beautiful with the smell of fresh blooming flowers, blue skies, and green fields. But in the spring of 1969 my world of colorful promises turned gray, ash gray, death's gray. It was as though God himself packed his bags, left town never to return, and Satan moved right in. I could feel the shadow of evil draping over me. The air turned putrid and it suffocated me. My heart stopped. My life stopped. Dean moved back from New Mexico and this time he stayed.

During the time Dean lived in New Mexico he joined a motorcycle gang. His second wife shared many stories with me about their time there. She told me the initiations into the motorcycle club were horrific and many had included her. The initiations included drugs, beatings, and rape. It's been almost forty years now since it happened and she says she still has nightmares.

She told me Dean eventually was accepted into the gang, but after some time had passed his arrogance surfaced and he tried to take control of the club. No matter what situation he got himself into he could not stand to be a follower. He needed to hold the reins of power. He reminded me of Hitler and was very persuasive and usually got his way. Dean needed to be number one, he would not, could not, settle for less. But the members of the club were not swayed, and for his attempt at mutiny they almost beat him to death and ran him out of town.

By the time Dean and his wife moved back to Kansas City, Mom was able to purchase a home. She was financially more secure by then with her well paying job and the VA benefits. Mom knew how to save money, and if she found a penny on the street she picked it up and put it in the bank. Being a bookkeeper she became obsessed when reconciling the books at work or her personal checkbook. She wanted to know that every penny she was responsible for or earned was safe. She would not walk away from reconciling when the money did not balance. The books could be off by a penny and she would spend hours checking and rechecking until they balanced. She was good at what she did and took pride in doing her job well.

The home Mom purchased was a beautiful red brick house with three bedrooms, one bath, a full basement and a one-car garage. It was a couple of miles away from Dora's house, but we were still in the same school system. Donna, Karl, and I were grateful for that.

After therapy Mom told me she had wanted to buy a house in Missouri. She said the three of us kids pitched such a fit at the thought of leaving our school and friends so she bought the red brick house. We never spoke the words to each other but it was evident the moment she told me that we both had the same thought. Slowly we looked up at each other, both of us with a half sad smile and a look of "what if." Softly shaking our heads side to side, wondering perhaps if we had moved to Missouri I may not have gone through the torture I endured while living in that house. But then again, I doubt a state line would have stopped him.

Dean and his second wife bought a house down the street from Dora's. I don't believe it was more than 800 to 1000 square feet if that much. It had two small bedrooms, one bath, a kitchen and living room. It was a small square house with no garage. Dean was into chopping motorcycles and showing them at the various car and motorcycle shows. He won a lot of trophies and they were piled around the inside of their small house. He spent a lot of money on his hobby, and I'm certain a lot of it was stolen or made from selling drugs.

Dean made decent money in the construction business but I don't believe he ever worked a full forty-hour workweek. He spent more time contemplating and pulling off his "next job" to make a quick buck. He often bragged about the robberies he pulled off stealing cars, motorcycles, and breaking into homes and businesses. Once he told me he and a few of his buddies stole a safe from a business, they brought it home and blew it up trying to open it. He carried weapons too and was always showing off a new gun he had stolen or purchased illegally.

Dean was proud of the heists he pulled off and he loved showing me the stolen goods before he sold or pawned his bounty. He was a full-fledged thug by the time he returned from New Mexico and he was taking drugs on a daily basis. I was told later he shot up using needles but I never personally saw him injecting anything. What I did witness for years was any drug he had in front of him he would devour it. It didn't matter what it was if you could snort it, smoke it or swallow it, he ingested it without thinking twice about it.

Shortly before the summer school break of 1969, I was standing in line with the other students waiting for my turn to board the bus to take me home from school. The drive was a big U shape with one way in and one way out. Waiting my turn to board the bus I could hear the roar of exhaust pipes screaming in the distant. I saw a three-wheeled motorcycle coming down the street and it turned screeching into the one-way drive fish tailing. Dean was showing off. He pulled up in front of the buses and sat there, looking cocky with his signature smirk on his face.

The paint job was a mixture of various colors of light and dark greens. The gas tank was painted with a naked lady sprawled across it. The front end was extended, all chrome, and he had ape hangers for the handlebars. The actual gas tank was behind the seat inside a steel beer keg.

I could hear the other kid's ewe and awe and there were sounds of excitement, *"Cool Man. Wow who's that?"*

Dean spotted me in the crowd and waved me over. I was excited he was asking me to join him. Smiling ear to ear, I started sprinting towards him. The kids were looking at me, and then back at him. He told me to jump on the back of the seat. I could hear the words of excited surprise coming from the other kids as I jumped on his tricked out three-wheeled bike and for a brief moment I felt cool.

Dean revved the throttle a couple of times. It was loud and we sped out of the school drive and down the street. I was shaking with excitement, all smiles, I felt special. My big brother came to pick me up on his motorcycle. I knew I was the envy of the kids at school. I was enjoying the ride thinking he was going to take me directly home. Instead, we pulled into the drive of his small square house.

Pulling up the drive, he turned and drove on the yard and parked in front of the door. We got off and went inside. I knew better than to sit in his chair so I sat on the couch. His wife was at work so it was just the two of us. He rolled a joint, lit it and said, *"I want you to try this."* He demonstrated how to take a hit and hold it deep in your lungs. I didn't want to. I went from feeling cool to terrified and he sensed it but he kept insisting. I had not even tried smoking cigarettes and he knew it. I don't remember what he said, I only remember his remarks made me feel stupid and cowardly because I was afraid to take a hit.

His power over me was hypnotic and I submitted, wanting to prove to him I was cool too. He handed me the joint looking at me with his blue eyes. They were full of self-indulgence. I took the joint out of his hand, slowly raised it to my lips, and took a hit. It felt as though I had inhaled fire and my throat and lungs burned. I coughed until I threw up. After I regained my composure he made me take another hit, and another and another.

When Dean moved to New Mexico he left a gangly silly little girl behind. When he moved back to Kansas City, he came back to a confident beautiful young woman. He saw my happiness, my success at school and my growing popularity and he would not stand for it. Dean could not stand to see any one excel in a positive way and that certainly included me. He was completely anti-establishment, and it seemed he was full of hatred towards anything good or pure. Dean was driven by absolute gluttony to extinguish the young woman I had blossomed into. He was determined to destroy and take away all of the happiness and confidence I had gained. That day he succeeded. Smirking with a sense of power, he stomped on my confidence and crushed me as if I were nothing more than a cockroach.

6

"Death is not the worst that can happen to men."

Plato (429 BC – 347 BC)

By the time school started in the fall of 1969 I was smoking pot on a regular basis. Dean kept me supplied with small bags of pot and rolling papers. Sometimes he would lace the pot with other drugs. He thought it was hilarious to see how completely wasted I would get. I would get beyond stoned, almost lethargic. Getting stoned was becoming a wonderful escape, and I started to really enjoy it.

By Christmas Dean was giving me LSD, acid, or mescaline. Some of the street names I remember were orange barrel or orange sunshine. I recall barrel shapes, round tabs, or sometimes the drug would be on small square piece of paper indicated by a dot on them. The drugs he gave me came in all shapes, sizes and colors. He would hand me something and I would swallow it, no questions asked. I was never sure if he was giving me uppers or downers, or if I was going on an acid trip. It was like going on a thrill ride; hold on tight because I was not sure what to expect.

I can not recall if I was nominated or not for School Queen the last year of Junior High. From age thirteen on it's hard to remember many details of my life perfectly. I was stoned from the ninth grade on. I do remember going to the Christmas dance that year in a beautiful dress. It was an empire dress, cranberry color velvet on top with a gold band and below the band the skirt was an off white cream color. I only remember because I have a couple of pictures of me wearing it.

Dean came by the house before I left for the dance. I felt beautiful all dressed up in my new dress, my hair and makeup were perfect. Mom left the living room and he held out his hand to give me something. Instinctively I held out mine too, palm up waiting for him to drop something in it. I was starting to recognize the drugs he gave me, that night it was a hit of acid. Without blinking, I raised it to my mouth and swallowed it.

I went to the dance not remembering how I got there or even remember leaving. I was twirling in the middle of the gymnasium, twirling and twirling and twirling. There were several Christmas trees in the gymnasium with beautiful lights of red, green, white and blue. No matter how fast I twirled everything was in slow motion and the lights swirled around me in one big circle. Fortunately, I never experienced a bad acid trip. Acid made everything beautiful, more vibrant and alive. I always went into an acid trip wanting to explore the high that was coming; it was exciting, a great escape. It was my moment of *Alice in Wonderland* and getting lost in my own world.

There is one thing I will always remember from that night, and it continues to haunt me to this day. A couple of guys noticed my peculiar actions and asked what was wrong with me. I was completely entrenched in the acid trip, laughing and my hands slowly reaching up and out, swaying in front of me trying to grab the beautiful colorful objects surrounding me. They thought I had lost my mind because there was nothing there. Giggling, I told the two of them I was stoned and told them what I had taken. I thought they would think I was cool but they didn't feel that way at all. They were mad at me for doing drugs, and for a brief moment I felt bad for being scolded by them. Laughing again, I shrugged my shoulders acting as if I didn't care what they thought and turned away from them. I wanted to dive deeper into that make believe rabbit hole I had created. It was my mad tea party and nobody was going to spoil it.

Not long after that night the two boys who scolded me at the dance were both into drugs and hanging out at Dean's house. I will never be able to prove it, but I believe Dean was solely responsible for bringing drugs into my neighborhood and introducing them to my friends. He preyed upon many of my friends, and most have not been as fortunate as I have been. Many lives have been completely destroyed or lost due to the drugs I believe he provided, my two male friends included. I have been informed that both of them are now dead from overdosing on drugs. I often find myself crying and grieving for all those lost souls.

Dean's house became a hangout for many of my school friends. We would smoke pot, drop acid, or do uppers or downers. He tried to get me to sell drugs for him. Thankfully I wasn't very good at it. Dean was luring all of us into his world, and there were many times he would give me drugs to share with my friends. He would give me grams of cocaine or PCP to take to school. I would sit in the back of a classroom cutting whatever it was into lines to share with my classmates. Before the bell rang to begin class, friends would come by my desk as if to say hello and snort a line.

I turned fourteen the following March. My appearance took a complete 180-degree turn. I wasn't bathing as often, my hair was long and stringy, and I would wear headbands, beads, and bell-bottom blue jeans. The school had a mandated dress code and I refused to abide by it. I just didn't care anymore. Many times while entering school I would be stopped at the front door and sent to the principles office. I would have to remove the beads and the headband and leave them at the office. I could retrieve them at the end of the day. By then I snubbed all school activities. I quit the drill team and softball. No one bothered to ask why.

Dean continued to show up at my school to give me a ride. Never knowing when he would come screeching down the school drive, it seemed he would show up just before the bus left the school. We always stopped at his house before he took me home. With Dean's wife working a full time job we were always alone in the house except when my friends would stop by.

The day my life completely descended into the darkest depths of despair began just like any other day. Dean picked me up from school and we stopped at his house to get stoned before taking me home. He went into the kitchen to get a beer and I noticed a motorcycle magazine on the side table. I picked it up and started thumbing through it. I was mortified at the pictures, but curiosity got the best of me and I kept looking. It was full of chopped out motorcycles and on every bike was a naked woman posing in suggestive positions. I wanted to act cool and grown up and tried not to show how embarrassed I was seeing the naked women. Dean came in the front room and sat close to me acting curious as to what I was looking at. I don't know how it began but we started talking about modeling. He was hinting that I could make a lot of money modeling. He said I was pretty enough and he had friends associated with the motorcycle magazine business so he could probably help me out.

The seduction started and, of course, I was clueless to his intentions and where all this was going. If I'd had any idea what he was up to I would have ran right out of his house and never looked back. He was as cunning as a snake oil salesman, skillfully relentless in his insistence that he could get me into a legitimate modeling job. I told him I didn't want to do any naked modeling and he assured me I wouldn't have too.

The thought of being a model and making money intrigued me. He said, *"I have a Polaroid maybe we could take a couple of shots. I will show them to my friends and see what they think."* Of course I thought "How fun."

His house didn't have a garage and he always parked his motorcycle in the living room. He suggested I sit on it and pretend I was driving. He took a couple of Polaroid shots. It seemed innocent enough and I was having fun posing. He starting rolling a joint and I noticed he sprinkled a white powdery substance on top of the pot before rolling it up. I was fourteen at the time and smoking pot with him on a regular basis was no big deal. I'm not sure what other drug he put in the joint but it was as if I was completely anesthetized. Continuing to reassure me that I could make a lot of money being a model, before I knew it I was completely naked and posing on the bike. Whatever he suggested I do, I did. Pulling the strings, posing at his command I was horribly scared, but for some reason I didn't want him to see my fear, so I complied without much hesitation.

His suggestions of different poses eventually led me to the bedroom. I don't remember what he said or how it happened, all I remember is lying on the bed and he was raping me, ripping my virginity from me. To this day I am sure my boyfriend at the time still believes he is the one who had the honor of deflowering me. Of course I couldn't tell him otherwise. Lying there paralyzed, like a zombie, I didn't understand what was happening and I could not look at him. His breath reeked of bear, cigarettes and pot, and the stench forced me to turn my face away from his.

I found something on the wall to focus on to help take me away from what was happening. Hanging there, on the wall, lifeless and forever burned into my memory, was a crucifix of Jesus.

The cross was black and the body of Jesus was silver. Studying every inch of his face, looking at the crown of thorns piercing into his head, I could see the outline of blood flowing down the side of his cheek. With his head hanging, Jesus looked completely defeated and utterly hopeless. I lay there feeling the same. I'm not sure why I didn't cry out loud, but in my head I was screaming and crying, "Jesus help me please, why aren't you helping me, why aren't you stopping him?" Just as Jesus was nailed to the cross, I was nailed to the bed and we were both completely powerless to stop what was happening. In the corner of his eye was a tear. Starring at it, I was thinking that Jesus was crying having to witness what was happening to me. Hanging there, He was forced to watch my brother commit the worst sin of all before Jesus took His last breath, *the sin of incest*.

I have never worn a cross around my neck, and I have never wanted to own any jewelry or art that has a crucifix. Seeing a cross or crucifix, I immediately flash back to that very moment and I must look away. Like a vampire condemned to a life of living hell I must look away because looking at a cross burns my soul at the mere site of it; another detail I have never shared with anyone, not even with my husband.

When I met my husband he was wearing a large gold mariner's crucifix with diamonds around his neck. I saw it and immediately looked away trying not to show the anguish I was feeling. I know he cherishes that piece of jewelry because he wears it often. When we first met, he shared with me that he had it made after his first wife died of cancer. It was made out of the wedding bands and other jewelry they wore during their marriage. I knew I would have to force myself to suck it up and not let him know how it made me feel. I was falling in love with him and I was determined not to ruin his cherished memories with my vile ugly ones.

I have trained myself to think about the love my husband had for his first wife and how cruel it was she died so young. I am almost afraid to even write about it now for fear that when he reads this he may never want to wear it again. Hopefully I know my husband better than that. He has seen me struggle with the aftereffects of the incest even after therapy and how I try not to let it control my life or me anymore. Now, determined when I see a cross, I look at it ever so fiercely just to prove the incest has no control over me. Perhaps because I do, in a way it still does.

I don't remember much else about that day, other than when Dean was finished with me I got dressed and sat on the couch. Stunned and dazed, I sat there trying to wrap my brain around what just happened. Or perhaps I was trying to forget it even happened, hoping it was all a nightmare. I was in complete shock not knowing what to say or what to do. Dean opened his wallet and handed me several folded dollar bills. Instinctively I reached out to take whatever it was he was handing me. I took the money from him, not looking at him or the money. I didn't count it, and I believe I even said, *"Thanks."*

He told me he would show the pictures to his friends and assured me they would like them, and this was payment up front. He said, *"I'm positive you will be able to make more money because you're so pretty, and better looking than the models in the magazine."* Stroking me, young and dumb and completely under his control I didn't question him. It was as if my mind left me. I was so stoned from the drugs he had given me all I could do was sit there in a daze and go along. I don't know why I never told anyone, perhaps because I took the money I felt responsible for what had just happened. By taking the money I was accepting *"It"* and *"It"* was ok. I didn't understand it at the time but he was buying my silence. His words and actions made me feel there was something special just between the two of us, and he continued to manipulate me, convincing me it was normal for him to do what he did to me. I worshiped him and I desperately wanted to believe him. I never questioned him even though it felt so wrong.

I'm not sure how much time went by, days, weeks, maybe months, and he told me his friends loved the pictures and wanted more. He said they offered to pay more money if I posed for more pictures and in more suggestive positions. He kept insisting and, completely stoned, I was posing again. He had his sex and afterwards handed me a wad of money. Years later I found out he never did sell the pictures to anyone. They were for his personal use only.

I don't remember how it came about but I was at Dean's house alone with his wife, and she was clearly upset about something. Before I knew what hit me she shoved the Polaroid pictures in my face and was demanding to know if I knew who was posing naked in the pictures. Of course I knew who it was! Clearly you could see my face, it was obvious they were pictures of me. I was wearing my boyfriend's class ring in the pictures. I looked down at my hand. I was wearing the same ring and tried to hide it. I acted stupid to her rhetorical questions and said I didn't know who it was and turned away from her. Her screaming and yelling about the pictures scared me at first, but getting caught that he had sex with me seemed to be more frightening. I'm not sure if I was afraid for my brother or me or for both of us that someone knew about our secret.

Soon after she confronted me she ended up in the hospital fighting for her life. My brother almost beat her to death. He told the family and his friends he caught her in bed with Black Sammy. That's not what they called him. Years later we would learn the truth of him beating her. Shortly after I told my mother I was in therapy for what Dean did to me, Linda now his ex-wife, called Mom to share some sad news with her. Twenty years earlier, around the same time Dean had taken those pictures, Linda was given a cat from one of Mom's best friends. She called Mom to tell her that the cat had passed away and Mom said, "*Well I have some horrible news too, Rena is in therapy.*"

Mom said there was a strange silence on the phone and, softly, Linda said, "*I know why.*" Mom said Linda's statement surprised her at first, then she suddenly remembered many years earlier someone telling her not to let Rena spend so much time with Dean and Mom asked, *"It was you wasn't it?"* Linda started crying and tearfully said, *"Yes it was me."* Mom said she almost fell to the floor she was so distressed to now know the meaning of her statement after so many years. Linda told Mom she had found the pictures he had taken of me and confronted him. He went completely mad and beat her, threatening to kill her if she ever told anyone. By trying to save my life Linda almost lost hers, and she lay at death's door for several days.

Mom told me that the two of them were completely overcome with grief about what happened to me. They spent hours on the phone trying to console each other, trying to understand how he could commit such evil. Linda had carried the burden of truth for years but had to keep her silence, or lose her life. After their conversation the burden of truth was passed to Mom and she stubbornly carried it for the remainder of her life. Seemingly, Mom wanted to torture herself for not understanding the insinuation of Linda's statement years ago. She felt like she failed as a mother by not protecting me. The burden of my abuse didn't belong to either of them. They were not at all responsible for what happened to me. Linda still apologizes to me because she feels she was not able to do more. It breaks my heart to see her sadness. Linda almost died trying to save me from Dean, and after their divorce she went through three years of therapy because of the horrible things he did to her.

I knew I could not tell anyone what Dean was doing to me at the time. I couldn't even admit it to Linda the day she showed me the pictures. Maybe I was afraid of what he would do to me should I betray him, and he would punish me as he had years ago in the back seat of the car. Deep down I knew what he was doing was wrong, but the more he manipulated my innocent mind and made me feel I was his special one I was able to shove the wrongness deeper and deeper each time it happened. Perhaps witnessing Linda's reaction I felt he would get in trouble. Hypnotically and completely bound to him, body and soul, the only thing anyone saw for years was how I blindly worshiped him. I had to protect him, protect us, unfortunately at all cost to me.

7

"Be gentle with the young."

Juvenal (55 AD – 127 AD)

I don't remember if I knew about Dean beating Linda at the time or not. If I did, I didn't understand the severity of the beating, or the real reason for it. I believe Dean and Linda were the only ones who knew the absolute truth of why he almost killed her. They had a very tumultuous marriage and she tried to leave him several times. Linda was just as hypnotically locked to him as I was. What we both thought was love was really an unquenchable brainwashed obsession of him.

Linda is a petite woman, two to four inches shorter than me, and very pretty with jet-black hair and dark eyes. Her hair and makeup are always perfect and she dresses beautifully. The moment I met her I was jealous of her. Cute and witty, the more she came around the more envious I became. She was seventeen when they started dating and Dean was twenty years old. I was nine at the time they met.

As soon as Mom and Linda hung up the phone Mom called me and said, *"Well you're never going to guess who I just spoke to."* Mom proceeded to share the complete conversation between the two of them and I was absolutely dumbstruck listening to Mom's reenactment of the phone call. After all those years I was finally hearing the truth. For years Dean feed us nothing but lies about Linda. I started crying, and I realized the ongoing jealousy I felt for Linda was unjustifiable.

Mom said Linda would like to talk to me if I wanted to. I said yes and she gave me her phone number. Linda and I spent hours on the phone talking about what he did to me, and the horrible things he did to her. She shared information about her years of therapy and I talked about the counseling I was receiving at the time. On the phone, Linda and I developed a strong bond and have been close ever since. Just recently Linda and I admitted that we were both jealous of each other. Looking back it was as though he intentionally played us against each other. He saw the jealousy between us and I'm sure it gave him great amusement to see how we both vied for his attention. I try to remember some of the things he did or said when the three of us were together, now it's obvious how he instigated situations just to have us compete for his attention.

Linda and I were talking recently and she shared a horrifying secret she carried with her all these years. I was fourteen at the time of her beating and after she recuperated she went back to Dean. Shortly after their reconciliation he tried to talk her into to having a three way with me. The moment she told me his desire I was so repulsed, and I could taste the vomit in my mouth. Still holding the phone, I fell to my knees with my hand over my mouth trying not to throw up. Linda was crying and telling me she had pleaded with him not to do such a vile thing. She kept repeating, *"She's only a child please leave her alone."* I was thinking, not only was I a child at the time but I was his sister, and he shouldn't have done the monstrous things he did to me in the first place. Apparently it wasn't long after he asked her to have a three way she was finally able to leave him. Letting her go, he never bothered her again.

I knew nothing of Dean's intentions for the three of us at the time. I cried with her and I thanked her over and over on the phone for not letting it happen. Linda still feels guilty for what happened to me. She feels she should have been more courageous in speaking out on my behalf. I try to remind her, no matter what she thinks she should have done to save me, the damage was done long before she found out about any of it.

Dean never approached me to pose for pictures after he beat her. I didn't know why, and I never asked why. I was happy he didn't have me pose for him anymore. Perhaps Linda confronting him sparked some sense of morality in him. But then again, that's a stupid thought. The pictures stopped but the sex and drugs continued. *"It"* didn't happen every day or week but *"It"* did continue. I never knew when it was going to happen, but it was sex drugs and rock-n-roll. "Love the one your with" he took literally.

Dean continued to pick me up from school. He continued to molest me, give me money and drugs, and then send me on my way. Every time he was finished with me it was becoming easier to act as if nothing happened and we would laugh and hang out and get stoned. No one ever had a clue what was going on. I became skillful at suppressing the pain of the incest. I could not allow myself to feel the pain of what was happening to me. I refused to feel the pain, and I became emotionally and physically numb to the whole situation. I wanted my life to be normal and happy, like I thought my friend's lives were. I became very clever at putting on a false face. I felt I must. After Linda's reaction to what he was doing to me I was even more terrified of anyone finding out.

Several months before I turned sixteen Dean purchased a pink Cadillac for me; anther form of payment that ensured my silence. Without question Mom refused to let me keep it, not to mention I didn't even have my driver's license yet. I became furious with Mom and started screaming and yelling that she didn't love me, that Dean was the only one who loved me. At the time I felt Mom was being selfish. Unfortunately, it was the final situation that led me to believe Dean was my only ally. Now completing an absolute inseparable bond, Dean and I were as one. It was just the two of us against the world and I continued to do whatever he demanded of me.

Shortly after my sixteenth birthday Mom noticed that my breasts were enlarging. She kept an eye on my periods and she noticed I hadn't used any feminine products for well over a month. I knew my breasts were getting larger and becoming more tender to touch but I had no clue as to why. However, Mom had her suspicions and confronted me. I admitted to having sex with my new boyfriend and she immediately made an appointment to see a doctor. Once it was confirmed I was pregnant she made an appointment with a different doctor.

Dean was twenty-seven when I became pregnant. As soon as he found out about the pregnancy he started teasing me in front of the family, dancing around the room pointing his finger laughing and smirking at me, repeating over and over "the rabbit died." I could not comprehend what it meant, but by the tone of his voice and the way he was acting I thought something horrible was going to happen to me. I was distraught enough having the knowledge of being pregnant, now a rabbit died and I was to blame. What the hell did a rabbit have to do with it anyway? Why was he insinuating I was an animal killer because I got pregnant? He kept teasing me, taunting me, calling me a slut and a little whore. I was scared and crying. I couldn't comprehend his behavior or understand why it was my fault a rabbit died.

Now, sadly but somewhat amusing, I understand the meaning of the dead rabbit. I also understand Dean's merciless excruciating actions that day. It was his way of diverting any suspicion away from him that he could possibly be the father. He was scared to death and he was frightening me to ensure my silence. If the family found out what he was doing to me the rabbit would not have been the only thing that died. He was terrified and he was siding with the other adults about what should be done about this undesirable situation. I felt alone and terribly scared, and I was concerned about my future.

Dean insisted he go to the doctor with Mom and I. He wanted to make damn sure I would get an abortion. Driving to the doctor's office, the two of them sitting in the front seat, they finalized the game plan I was to follow. Mom and Dean felt if I followed their instructions completely it would ensure the Doctor would agree to give me an abortion. It was 1972 and the Roe v. Wade court case did not take place until the following year in 1973. Before that landmark decision there was a lot of red tape women went through to get an abortion in Kansas. During that time legalized abortions were performed in the hospital under anesthesia, but only if the doctor felt it was the right course of action in each particular case.

When we finally met with the doctor he was sitting behind his desk, dressed in his long white coat wearing a shirt and tie. He sat with his elbows resting on the arms of the chair, his hands clasped with his fingers intertwined, and his thumbs were tapping together. He wore glasses, which were hanging on the end of his nose. His eyes, smug and condescending, were peering over his glasses looking down upon me, not directly at me. The three of us sat in individual chairs in front of his desk. Mom and

Dean, legs crossed shoulders stern and determined, were sitting totally annoyed with me for putting them in this predicament. It didn't seem to matter what I was going through. Mom was not about to let this man, this doctor, intimidate her just because of his position, so she sat there composed and unyielding. I sat between the two of them and my head hung so low my chin was resting on my chest. My eyes were red and swollen from crying. Slumped in my chair I felt very small, ashamed and dirty.

I was doing my best to do as I had been instructed. I tried to look at the doctor when he spoke to me. In an unsympathetic, intimidating, tone of voice he asked, *"Well Rena, tell me why you want to have an abortion?"* Feeling scared, not able to give him my true answer, I repeated the words Mom and Dean had decided upon, *"Well Sir I don't want to have a baby. I made a horrible mistake, and my boyfriend took advantage of me. I want to go to college after I finish High School. If I have a baby I will not be able to."* It was that simple.

The next thing I knew I was waking up in a hospital recovery room. Groggy and trying to focus, having awakened from the anesthesia, I started crying uncontrollably and yelling, *"I want my baby, I want my baby."* A nurse ran over to me and viscously spat out under her breath, *"Be quiet your disturbing the other patients."* I continued to cry but shoved my face into the pillow. I was in pain both physically and emotionally. I was hysterical. The situation was cold and uncaring and it seemed the procedure was nothing more than cutting out a cancerous tumor from my body. Once the abortion was completed there was no need to discuss it any further. As usual, my family went about their lives as if nothing out of the ordinary had happened.

From the moment my pregnancy was discovered it was determined by everyone in the family I would have the abortion. No one ever asked me what I wanted. Mom didn't care what I wanted, she was adamant that I would not have a baby at sixteen. I stayed in bed for several days. Neighbors and friends were told I had the flu, and I should not be disturbed or they could possibly become infected. My boyfriend knew the truth about my pregnancy but he was not allowed to visit me. He was turned away every time he tried.

Mom was pro abortion all the way, she didn't care what the circumstances where. If a woman wanted an abortion it was her body and she should be able to have one if she wanted. But this wasn't her body it was mine, and she gave me no choice in the matter. I was to have the abortion, period. It would be years later when I found out why she was so insistent I have an abortion.

I was in my early to mid-twenties and lived in a studio apartment. My apartment was on the top floor of an eight story building which was built around 1930 or 1940. It was almost midnight and I was asleep. Someone was persistently bussing from the front door to come up. It was Dean, and he was crying and yelling. I asked him why he was upset and he told me he had located his father and talked with him on the phone. Mom told us after her divorce from Dean's father she didn't know what happened to him or where he had moved. Dean said he confronted him and asked why he divorced Mom, leaving him behind, and never tried to contact him. Dean said his father started laughing and said, *"Divorced? I was never married to your mother. I didn't want anything to do with her. She pursued me, got pregnant, and wanted me to marry her. I didn't want to marry her. Besides, she was married at the time."*

There it was, Mom's secret, she had an affair during WWII with Dean's father while her first husband was away fighting in the war. Dean kept ranting, *"I'm a bastard child they weren't even married."* He told me he just left Mom's house and he cussed her out for lying to him all those years. I immediately got dressed and told him to leave because I was going to Mom's house to check on her. Dean was incensed that I was concerned about her and not consoling him about his shocking news. The more he kept going on about him being an illegitimate bastard child the more enraged I was becoming. I couldn't take it anymore and I screamed at him, *"So what's the big deal, she could have given you up for adoption but she obviously didn't."* My heart was sinking and I thought, "Oh God, how I wished she had!" As usual it was all about him, he didn't give a damn about Mom or the anxiety she was suffering now that we knew about her secret.

I drove as fast as I could to get to Mom's house. It seemed it took hours to get there but it was only a twenty-minute drive. I ran into the house. Donna and Karl were standing at the side of her bed looking worried and at a complete loss on how to console her. Mom was as white as the sheets on her bed. Her eyes were hollow and red and she looked so lifeless lying there. She was panic-stricken and barely able to speak. She kept repeating over and over, *"I just want to die, I just want to die."* She was embarrassed that we found out she had been lying to us all those years, and she was sinking deeper into a state of depression. We were told Mom had been married four times when in reality it was only three. The four of us were crying by then. Sitting next to her on the bed I grab her hand, held it to my chest, and said, *"No Momma its ok. You have nothing to be ashamed of."*

Mom proceeded to tell her side of the story. Dean's father pursued her and promised to marry her. She was lonely and with her husband off fighting in the war she worked long hours to support her and her first two children, Punkin and Butch. He promised he would take care of all three of them. He charmed the pants right off Mom and all was good until she became pregnant. The moment he found out about the pregnancy he left town and she never heard from him again.

Mom told me she thought about giving Dean up for adoption but her mother talked her into keeping him. I am almost certain if abortions were legal when she became pregnant with Dean she would have had one. She said Grandma Marsh wanted Mom to keep him and she would help her take care of him. Mom divorced her first husband. I was told he loved Mom no matter what and didn't want the divorce. After Dean was born Mom felt she had no choice, she had betrayed her husband and felt she must divorce him. I think the real reason was because she fell deeply in love with Dean's father and no longer loved her husband. Perhaps that's the real reason she kept Dean, because it was the only part of his father she could hold on to.

Donna, Karl and I spent the night with Mom to make sure she was going to be ok. That was the first time I ever saw Mom so broken and frightened. The second time was years later, the day I told her I would write this book. She was right to be concerned about telling my story, she knew that by sharing my secrets I would also have to tell hers. We never spoke about that night ever again. As usual we went about our lives as if nothing out of the ordinary happened. I did it mainly because I knew how embarrassed Mom was that we knew about the affair and I was determined not to make her feel uncomfortable or ashamed. It made me realize how human she really was and I felt somewhat empowered, but sad knowing she had such a painful secret too.

In family conversations we still talk as though Mom had been married four times. I know she was grateful we kept her secret within the family. Her friends and acquaintances knew nothing of her secret, perhaps only the ones she might have told. Most of her friends have passed away so I don't feel like I am betraying her to write about the truth now. Mom was a strong determined woman, not letting anything get her down, but I believe that was one secret she wished she could have carried to her grave.

8

> *"Those who can make you believe absurdities*
> *can make you commit atrocities"*
>
> **Voltaire** (1694 - 1778)

I didn't receive any form of counseling before or after my abortion. No one really knew how much grief and sadness I was carrying in my heart. I couldn't even share my feelings with my best friend Dora. Not being offered any counseling to help me deal with the trauma of the abortion was a horrible injustice to me, and afterwards I didn't give a damn about anything. I was lost, but mostly I felt damaged.

To family and friends I acted as though everything was ok. Actually I was a severely tormented soul. I did whatever I could to suppress the pain. All the drugs Dean supplied me with seemed to help somewhat. However, no matter how hard I tried to hold in the anger there were times my pain would surface, like a boil festering to the point of bursting open. The anger would spew from my lips. Ranting and screaming I would make declarations such as: *"I will never have children! Why bring a child into this world of hate and ugliness? There is nothing to be happy about or to live for."* I would rage on and on with remarks similar to those and people were confused and disgusted by my bleak public statements. But they didn't take the time to understand why I would say such drastic things.

Being treated so coldly as I was before, during and after the abortion, unfortunately lead me down an even more destructive path. I became very promiscuous in High School, going from boy to boy searching for someone to love me, to care for me. I wanted to be loved. I didn't necessarily want sex, but in order to be loved by men I was conditioned to believe giving them sex would make them fall in love with me. I wanted to feel love, from someone. Anyone!! Ironically, even when I did find someone who truly wanted to love me I was unable to open my heart to him. Being treated properly, respectfully, was foreign to me. I rejected both them and their kindness. What they tried to offer me did not feel real, it felt fake. But most of all, I felt that I didn't deserve to be treated nicely. I didn't know what true love felt like. I only knew how to accept abuse, sexually, physically and emotionally. Sadly, that's how I thought true love came packaged.

Being forced by my family, mainly Mom, to act as though the abortion never occurred, along with the years of sexual abuse, I believe all of it contributed to my increasing risky sexual behavior and self-abuse. Over the years, even with birth control so easily available, more often than not I didn't use any, on purpose. I just didn't give a damn. I didn't deliberately set out to, but I did come to use abortion as a form of birth control. Determinedly, I did use it as a form of punishment. Why not? That's what I was taught to do. When I was forced to have my first abortion I felt I was being punished. Over the years I used abortion several times to punish myself. I became so emotionally and psychically numb perhaps it was a way to feel alive. To feel pain in any form made me feel I was still part of this earth and not lost in the darkness of my personal nightmare. After awhile I even became numb to the abortions. They became so matter of fact, so routine, as if it was nothing more than going to the dentist to get my teeth cleaned.

Deep down I felt I had to punish myself, I didn't feel worthy enough to bring life into this world, and I didn't deserve to be a mother. It is difficult at times to think about, and I try not to have any regrets of the choices I have made through the years. Whether the choices I made were out of ignorance or due to the control of the incest, I absolutely take full responsibility for everything I have done. However, at times I do get small twinges of pain pulling at my heart. Longing to be loved by a child or loving one, I often daydream about growing old and not having children or grandchildren. But those tugs of pain in my heart immediately subside when I see a young mother struggling to take care of her children financially, or if the children are misbehaving. At that moment I am brought back to my own reality and mostly content with my life as it is. Thankful I had a choice and grateful for things as they are. I have to be. Regrets can slash holes in your soul that can never be mended.

When Mom became more involved with her work and her social activities, she felt Dean was looking after us. His hanging around more than usual lead her to believe he was. He was looking after us all right!! My pregnancy scared the hell out of him and he left me alone for a while. He was not picking me up from school anymore mainly due to the fact that before the abortion Mom had given me a car for my sixteenth birthday. It was a white Corvair with red interior and was in mint condition. I drove it to school every day and, fortunately, Dora was with me most of the time and I felt safe. Eventually Dean would feel the need to inflict his many forms of abuse on me and would come to the red brick house searching for me. He would come up with some excuse for me to join him on his errand.

People often wonder why I didn't stop Dean from abusing me. It is hard for me to understand too, let alone make them understand. But there were times he treated me as his kid sister. Some trips I was allowed to tag along with my big brother and we actually had fun together. He would take me to meet his friends. We would go to his favorite hangouts and I would sit and watch him drink while he joked around with his buddies. I felt he was showing me off and acting proud of me. Each trip was shrouded in mystery of what the outing might entail. I was always walking on eggshells. Was I going to be molested on this trip or was he going to leave me alone? The outings he didn't molest me were fun and made me crave more of those times with him. Each trip I would go hoping for the best, it was always a toss of a coin.

Upon returning home from our trips Donna and Karl would be waiting and craving attention from him as well. When they saw the two of us together, laughing and having fun, it would create such a strain between the three of us younger siblings. They had no idea my laughter was fabricated to suppress the pain I was feeling. Some days the laughter was of relief and I was happy because nothing had happened on that particular outing. Flaunting his special treatment of me, Dean would yell at them to clean up the house or emotionally abuse them, making them both feel worthless. His negative comments only increased their jealousy towards me, especially Donna. He was brutal to her and it was obvious she just wanted the same attention from him she thought I was receiving.

I began to act out toward others in hateful ways. I was boiling over with anger and had to release the rage somewhere, anywhere, so I started bullying girls. My friends and school acquaintances became my target. I hated being vicious and didn't like how I was acting, but it seemed I couldn't control it. Some of my despicable actions have been removed from my memory, perhaps from the drugs or, most importantly, because I hated how I treated others.

The summer of 2009, thirty-five years after graduation, I connected with two of my Junior and High School girlfriends. Meeting for lunch, after so many years, one woman told me how I beat the holy crap out of her. I was saddened to hear her story because I have only the fondest memories of her. As she continued with her story I began having flash backs and realized she was telling the truth. I had completely blocked the memory of what I did to her. I began to feel sick to my stomach and I begged her forgiveness. She graciously accepted my apology and forgave me, and we continued with our visit. I still feel horrible about what I did to her. I bullied several girls during my Junior and Senior High School years. Some things I remember and some I'm sure I do not.

Recently Dora shared a story I had completely forgotten as well. During her sophomore year a couple of girls I hung around with started bullying her. They took her jean jacket from her and she came to me for help. I approached them and demanded they give her jacket to me or I would beat the crap out of them. They were both deathly afraid and handed the jacket to me. I made it absolutely clear to everyone that Dora was my best friend and no one was to ever touch her. Right after that incidence I threatened my locker partner, kicked her out and moved Dora in. No one ever bothered her again.

When Donna started High School she was grateful I had left such a legacy of being a bully. Over the years she told the story several times that when the other kids in school found out I was her big sister, they were nice to her and spared her from any harassment. Always laughing and swelled with pride whenever she shared her story, she would thank me for being a bully allowing her to enjoy school without being harassed. Looking back, I wish I could have protected her better. I wish I could have been more than just a bully for her. I didn't like being mean to people, but I felt if I were a bully no one would bother me.

If all those girls really knew the truth, and that I was fearful of them, they would have laughed at my weakness and beaten the holy crap out of me. I was insecure and scared but I couldn't show it for fear of being terrorized. The pain of the abuse was raging inside me and I felt I must penalize others. I was mimicking Dean, punishing everyone who stumbled onto my path. The bullying I do remember, I secretly felt horrible about afterwards. I never admitted that to anyone. I'm not sure why but I could not appear weak to anyone, ever. There is no excuse for bullying and I hope I will have the chance to apologize to all those girls I might have harmed. I will have to take their word for it because I don't remember who I tormented. After a while I stopped terrorizing people. I hated being cruel to others. The rage needed to be directed at someone and eventually that person turned out to be me.

Unfortunately, I learned that day at lunch that Dean's control of me went far beyond sexual. My High School friends shared another story with me. It completely brought me back to the world of darkness I have tried so hard to leave in the past. She told me that Dean went to my school and talked a girlfriend of mine into going for a ride on his motorcycle. He drove her to the red brick house. Dean made me show her the pictures he'd taken of me, perhaps promising her a future in modeling. She told my friend at the table the pictures frightened her. She made some excuse to leave and ran home. Listening to the story, I dropped my fork and put my hand over my mouth. I became physically ill and started shaking. I kept saying, *"Oh My God, Oh My God I don't remember doing that."* But the way I felt in my gut I knew it was true. As the day went on, and several days after, I continued having sickening flash backs of that appalling day so long ago.

Neither of the women at lunch knew any details of my abuse. They just found out earlier the same year about my story of incest and my desire to write this book. How could anyone make up such a story? The only people who knew about the pictures were Dean, Linda, and I, and I never told anyone. I was getting sick to my stomach and couldn't finish my meal. I started to cry. I asked my friend to please call her that very day and tell her how truly sorry I was. Witnessing how upset I was by what she just shared, my friend felt badly for relaying the story and, in a way, I wish she hadn't. I was ashamed to hear what I did to her. Sickened by my participation in such an evil act, I couldn't bring myself to call her directly and apologize.

The story confirmed how vile my brother really was and how he had complete control over me. That day at lunch I was innocently forced to remember how he tried to use me to molest my friend. Flashing fragments of memories I had managed to push deep inside kept bombarding my conscious mind for the remainder of the day. I couldn't block the memories no matter how hard I tired and it made me feel dirty and ashamed all over again. I was so repulsed and felt if he weren't dead already I would kill him myself.

The girl who saw those pictures that day, so long ago, told my friend that Dean didn't molest her. I hope and pray it's the truth, but it makes me wonder if any of my friends were one of his victims. It never dawned on me before that day my brother was a pedophile and the thought made me hate him even more. To commit such horrid ugly acts on me wasn't enough, he used me to lure other prey into his den of seduction. He made me an accomplice in his immoral acts and the knowledge of that made me physically ill.

Securing my involvement as his partner in crime insured my share of the responsibility. Perhaps that's another part of the convoluted incest equation and why I never told anyone. I felt responsible for what was happening to me and for the things he made me do. He manipulated me into thinking everything he did to me and everything I did to myself was at my own doing, my own fault. He was so cunning! Manipulating me into believing I was solely accountable seemed to relinquish any responsibility on his part and, therefore, his actions were justified in his mind. I believe he felt he did nothing wrong to me or anyone else.

Not long after Dean's death, in January of 2009, I went to visit his son Michael. Searching through some of his belongings we found a journal. One ending in his written thoughts was, "I am still in awe of the woman who directed the demise of life as I knew it. Guess I'll do a blast, I will not cop to being an addict just because I slam." He mentioned

Florida and I knew he was writing about me. Years after the truth came out, still hooked on drugs, he would not take any responsibility for what he did to me. He blamed me for his demise, living and dying alone in squalor. He blamed me for everything.

During therapy I accepted responsibility for my part of the incest and the years of self-abuse and forgave myself. However, eighteen years after therapy to hear the stories of what I did to those women years ago was very hard for me to accept. I wonder how many more memories are hidden away in my mind and might surface in the coming years. I hope there are no more forgotten secrets. I can only pray that all of the secrets are out of my head and I will not be bombarded with memories as horrible as those. Only time will tell.

Another revelation has come to pass; all these years I thought I had only suppressed the pain of what happened to me. The past several months, since meeting with my friends over lunch, I have come to terms that I suppressed memories as well. I have been trying to piece together the pictures of forgotten moments that battered my mind during lunch and the days that followed. I had never experienced memory flash backs, now I understand the women and men who have shared their stories and their experiences. It is physically and mentally incapacitating. The abuse I inflicted on others was so painful, so unfathomable at the time, the only way to cope was too suppress the memory of it, block it out, and throw it away as far away as possible.

I tried to keep it together at lunch that day. I was afraid to let my friends know how horribly distressed I was at hearing their stories. They knew their tales of long ago upset me but I didn't want to completely break down in front of them. Getting into my car and driving away, knowing they were out of sight, I broke down emotionally. I was so tormented by the stories they shared with me. I pulled the car into a parking lot and screamed and cried. I was crying so hard, gasping for air, it was difficult to breathe. The memories started surfacing and I couldn't control them. The pain and truth of the memories kept pounding over and over me like waves of a tsunami and it seemed to never end. I felt like I was drowning in a sea of pain.

When I called for help years ago, I mentally prepared myself to deal with the incest and the painful experiences I knew I would endure to work through it all. Having flashbacks is a painful, sickening, experience, and there is no way to mentally prepare for the feelings they conjure up. They surface unexpectedly from hearing a story or a sound, or maybe a song on the radio might strike a nerve. Gut wrenching flashbacks start shooting at you as if you're tied to a pole in front of a firing squad and you can't move. You're forced to remember something you tried so hard to forget and it is excruciatingly debilitating.

I have been working through these experiences and learning how to forgive myself once more. These past few months I seem to have slipped back into the darkness and I hate it. I have more healing to do. I'm so angry that I feel this way again. I thought I had been "healed." I thought I was free from Dean and free from the incest. Now I stop and breathe because I can choose how to look at all of it. Since therapy I try to turn negative experiences into positive lessons. In my heart I know I am no longer a victim and I want to be completely free of him and the incest. I know the only way to reach my absolute potential of happiness and peace is to get all of the toxic waste of the abuse out of me. I cannot and will not allow him to have control over me again. I must forgive myself again for the memories that have surfaced, to not do so gives him a power he no longer has.

9

After my abortion Mom had no clue I was becoming more sexually active or turning into such a horrible creature. When she was home I would act as if nothing were out of the ordinary. We never had any heart to heart talks and we certainly didn't talk about the abortion or what I was doing with my life. It was shoved under the rug with all the other family secrets. Mom acted as though the abortion never happened and I was supposed to do the same. Perhaps she thought after experiencing the pain I had endured I might somehow, magically, stop having sex. Mom was in denial, and she immersed herself in her job and was becoming more active in several women's clubs and dating occasionally.

She was paying less attention to the three of us still living at home. She suffered from what I call Ostrich Syndrome: keep your head buried in the sand and things will supernaturally fix themselves and you won't have to deal with them.

Mom, now financially independent, had no intention of ever remarrying. She was enjoying both her freedom and the feminist opportunities of that era. Mom gave birth to my older sister Punkin in 1941 when she was nineteen, and she gave birth to my youngest brother Karl in 1962 when she was forty. I'm sure Mom wasn't tired of sex, but she was definitely tired of having children. It was the sixties and women were burning their bras and enjoying their sexual freedom. After Mom's hysterectomy I think she too was enjoying her sexual freedom.

Mom grew tired of being oppressed by a male dominated society and she spent more time in her women's activities and was rarely home. I had more freedom to do as I pleased, and I did. Mom was a good provider and I know she loved us because she kept us fed and clothed, but she was not at all nurturing. Mom came home every night but never checked to make sure we finished our homework or talked about our day at school. She did make sure we had something to eat and our clothes were clean and we had a warm bed to sleep in.

My mother was not an affectionate woman and she had a hard time hugging anyone, even her own children. We were the ones who would initiate any affection and wait for her to reciprocate. I remember when my Grandma Groom died I was upset and crying. I was named after her, "Rena," and I loved her dearly. Mom was sitting in her chair and I kneeled before her crying and put my head in her lap. I desperately needed her to comfort me, hoping she would say something to soothe me or wrap her arms around me. A pat on the head, and a "there, there it will be all right" would have sufficed. Moments went by, nothing happened: she was stone cold, she didn't flinch a muscle, no hand on my head, no words of comfort. After several minutes I got up and walked away. I was devastated she didn't offer to console me and I started crying because of her indifference. I'm not sure why, but I couldn't tell her how much she had hurt me by her coldness. I was in a state of shock and speechless that she didn't offer any comforting motherly support.

Over the years Mom told us the story of how her mother treated her when her father passed away. Punkin recently reminded me of her story and hearing it once again made me realize Mom's coldness that day somehow made sense. Mom was seven years old at the time of his death and was very close to her father. She was devastated he had left her. It was 1929 and his appendix had ruptured. Gangrene set in and took his life. Penicillin had been discovered the year before and could have prevented his gruesome death. However, its healing powers weren't known at the time of his infection, and it wasn't used medically until a year after his death in 1930.

Mom wanted to go to the funeral but her mother didn't want to take her. Grandma Marsh relented only after her family's continued persistence that she should take Mom to say goodbye to her father. Standing side by side and looking into the coffin Mom told us Grandma Marsh looked down at her and coldly said, *"The only person in the world who ever loved you is laying right there, and he's dead now."* She forcefully grabbed Mom by the hand and dragged her home. That was that. Mom was right when she told us Grandma Marsh was not only a crazy old woman but was heartless too.

I know Mom loved us dearly but it was obvious being affectionate or nurturing was foreign and very difficult for her. She shared how she was neglected and never received any affection or nurturing from her mother or anyone after her father's death. I don't think Mom wanted to be so cold, perhaps she was just afraid to show any affection. Actually, I just don't think she knew how to. It was easier for Mom to demonstrate her love like a lioness protecting her cubs. If she knew we were in any immediate danger or someone was trying to harm us, metaphorically speaking, she would lunge at the neck for an instant kill. Mom wasn't afraid of anyone when it came to her children and she would physically and verbally stand up to anyone.

After she became a Grandmother she tried hard to become more loving and affectionate. I could see how she desperately wanted to be more warm-hearted by outwardly caring and hugging her grandchildren, but she struggled with it. Over the years we all learned to accept what she could give and savored the brief gifts of affection whenever they would surface.

It was by pure coincidence Dean knocked on her front door the day after I called Mom and told her I was in therapy because of the incest. He was in town from California,

I don't remember why, I think it was for a friend's funeral and he simply stopped by to visit with her. Peering out the window to see who was knocking, Mom opened the door and stood firmly in the doorway blocking his entrance. Ferociously spitting out these words she said, *"I know what you did to Rena through the years and I WILL NEVER forgive you!"*

Mom said she stood her ground determined to make Dean aware of just how monstrously evil his betrayal was to her and the family, but most importantly to me. She said she did not utter another word and stood there unwavering to show him she would make him pay for the insurmountable damage he did to me. Mom said his response was bluntly arrogant, and he showed no remorse that she had found out what happened to me. Shrugging a shoulder and with his signature smirk Dean said, *"Well there are two sides to every story. Is there anything you want me to have because I won't come back?"* Mom furiously said, *"I can't think of a damn thing,"* and slammed the door in his face. She never saw him again.

The following day was a Monday. Not wasting any time by making an appointment, pacing and waiting for the doors to open at 8:00 am, she marched into her lawyer's office and had his name irrevocably removed from her will. She spent the day going to the bank and other financial institutions to have Dean's name removed from all other documents pertaining to any gifts of inheritance. That was her way of going for the kill, disowning him, and protecting the rest of her children. Dean was so egotistical and always felt more entitled to any inheritance than the rest of us. Many times over the years he made no qualms letting the family know of his entitlement, especially after he found out Mom was not married to his Father. He felt she owed him deeply. Mom knew eradicating him from our lives was the only way she could possibly hurt him for what he did to me and for his betrayal to the family. She would never forgive him and would make him pay.

The moment Mom told me what Dean said to her that day, and not showing any remorse, I felt a sudden lightness in my soul and the weight of the guilt I had been carrying for telling the truth was lifted from my shoulders. I felt victorious because in that one sentence he admitted to everything, but he would not take any responsibility for any of it. He was basically telling Mom I was a willing participant from the age of four and not to blame him for any wrongdoing.

Later the same day Dean went to Mom's he called and left a message on my answering machine and said indignantly, *"I can't believe you would hurt our Mother like that."* I was outraged to hear his voice and I threw the phone across the room. He had the audacity to blame me for breaking Mom's heart by telling her the truth. He didn't give a damn about Mom he was only concerned about how it was all going to play out for him. I don't even think it bothered him that the family wanted nothing more to do with him, he was only concerned about his potential inheritance. I'm not sure why, but I kept the tape with his message on it.

The moment I heard his voice on my answering machine I realized I had spent decades wasting so much energy protecting him. I was completely brainwashed from the years of his manipulation. I spent years protecting a man that convinced me, programmed me, to believe he was the only one who loved me and what he did to me was not wrong.

It was a huge "ah ha moment!" The absolute awareness and clarity to come to terms with the shear torture he forced upon me for years made me mad as hell! The amount of energy it took every day to hide what he was doing to me was exhausting and day after day it stripped me of who I was, and who I was supposed to become. Even after the molestation stopped I had to continue the façade for years and it was grueling to keep up the pretense. I expended so much energy every day protecting him and our secret there was nothing left in me. I could not look past the next day or even believe there was a tomorrow for me to look forward too. It took every bit of concentration and energy I had just to survive through the day at hand.

For years I was in a perpetual state of make believe, day after day, and it was draining the light from my soul. I had to pretend I was a happy child: pretend we had a healthy normal brother-sister relationship; pretend I wasn't harboring any deep dark secret that was in control of me. I never had the strength to envision what I wanted to be or could be when I grew up, nor was I ever encouraged to do so. I could only imagine healthy children spending their days playing, as children should, and fantasizing about what they wanted to be when they grew up. I never had the time or energy to think about growing up.

Surviving each day emotionally was always my main focus. Unable to think about any tomorrows my thoughts were of the moment trying to make it through each day, trying to stay ahead of the confusion of what was happening to me. Looking for acceptance and to be loved meant complying with and tolerating what Dean and the others demanded of me. By doing so I thought I was loved. Being Dean's special one, his plaything, was all I thought my life was going to be. Perhaps that's another connection to answering the question of why the abuse went on as long as it did. For the longest time I didn't think my life was to be anything other than what was happening to me.

From the age of four until the day I went into therapy at the age of thirty-four my days were spent acting happy and in control, shoving the pain deeper and deeper inside me. Dean's control made me push my life aside and only be concerned with how he would be hurt if the truth ever came out. I was driven by fear every day to act as if my life was normal, whatever normal is. I was always fearful of how I would be blamed for everything, not him, and the fear and shame drained me of my energy. I couldn't concentrate on anything else.

After graduating from High School in 1974 I struggled with my life and my career choices. I spent a couple of years jumping from retail positions to various office jobs. When I was finally able to say "NO MORE" to Dean I knew I must do something with my life. I was tired of being under his control. It was scary but I ventured out and I enrolled in a Junior College. Even after taking a few classes, I was still not certain what career path I should embark upon. I didn't finish college, I couldn't get through algebra. I'm not a big fan of math, and it was a convenient excuse for not finishing school. I could have hired a tutor but I was just stumbling through my life not sure which direction I should or could go.

Somehow I stumbled into a sales career. Thankfully, people have come into my life that had faith in me, even when I could not believe in myself. With lots of persuasion from many people I was learning how to recognize opportunities when they came my way, but I was cautious of their intentions. I could not trust anyone. I was fearful of my own ability and felt undeserving. Not certain if I was more afraid of success or failure. In the late 1980's my sales career began to take off. After therapy, with my newly found confidence personally and professionally, I began to soar. I enjoyed a long and successful sales career in the construction industry until the building boom went bust in the early 2000's.

I met my husband in 1996 before the economic bust, when the building industry was prosperous. We were attending the same trade show for the construction industry and not long after the day we met I knew he was the one I was going to marry. I knew I would have to tell him what happened to me before he proposed. I wanted to give him an easy out before the proposal in case he couldn't handle all of my family secrets.

I shared my story of abuse from my brother and the others, but I didn't offer any details. I didn't need to. Just telling him I was sexually abused infuriated him. He looked at me with such pain and sorrow in his eyes and said,

"My God, just think what you could have accomplished had those things not happened to you."

He was probably right, but I felt he was looking at me as the proverbial glass that is half empty. Financially I was very successful and I was happy and proud of where I was in my life. I had climbed many hurdles to get to where I was and I was in a good place. I was pleased with my life, financially secure, and never dreamed my life could be so good. I couldn't allow him to diminish my life and the journey it took to get where I was at that moment in my life.

I looked him directly in the eyes and sternly said, *"NO, you cannot look at me that way. I may not be the person I am today had I not gone through what I have."* And I meant every word of it. I was adamant and made him understand I was not looking for any pity, ever. I told him I look at myself as a glass half full, and every day my glass was filling up with endless opportunities and I was in a good place.

Because of his reaction to my story the clarity of my life's purpose was at hand even more than before and I was secure about what I wanted to do with my life. That's when I revealed my intentions of writing this book to share my story, hoping it may help other victims of incest and child abuse. I wasn't exactly certain of my course, but I knew I must share my story with the world and I wanted him to know exactly what he was in for. Three months later he proposed and we were married a year later.

Both Dean's admission to Mom and leaving his accusatory message on my machine released me from the burden of guilt for telling the truth. I stopped feeling guilty about Mom and my other brothers and sisters banishing him from the family and wanting no more contact with him. The emotions began pouring out of me and I knew I was on my path to healing. I was angry but resolute and I wasn't going to take it anymore. Determined to deal with whatever I had to in order to reclaim my life, I was purposeful to reach as far into that deep dark hole I was living in, find "ME," and pull myself out of the darkness.

Getting angry was the beginning of my journey to a healthy life, and realizing I spent all those years wasting precious moments protecting Dean kicked my butt into high gear. I always feared the repercussions from Dean and feared what would happen to him if I told the truth. To now realize that he was nothing more than a smug spineless coward incensed me beyond belief. Also, recognizing that he had robbed me of my childhood and the years that followed really made me mad.

My healing began in earnest that day, an unintentional gift from him. Being a coward by not accepting any responsibility of the incest was the only good thing he ever did for me. It made me mad as hell and even more determined to reclaim my life. I felt empowered for the first time ever, and I started dancing around my apartment laughing and shedding tears of joy and sadness. I was free from the guilt of telling the truth. I knew I would have many more emotional hurdles to climb over but it was a good day, and it was the first day of the rest of MY new life.

10

"Courage conquers all things."

Ovid (43 BC – 17 AD)

I'm not sure how long I had the white Corvair, one or two years and then it was totaled. Dora and I were driving around and were stopped at a red light laughing and joking around, when all of a sudden we were hit from behind. The Corvair was pushed into the car in front of us and that car was pushed into two more. It was a five-car pileup. The force broke our bucket seats and we were thrown into the dash. There were no seat belts in the car. The car that hit us didn't brake at all. The Police said the car was traveling approximately thirty-five to forty-five MPH and we were fortunate the engine was in the back of the car. It had protected us from most of the impact. We were sore and

shaken by the experience but fortunate there were no broken bones or lacerations.

After the car was totaled it opened the door for Dean to
start meeting me after school again. Sometimes he would
show up with a girlfriend and I would ask if my boyfriend
or a friend could ride along. Sometimes he allowed me to
bring someone but if he wanted to be alone with me he
would say no.

If I dated a boy Dean didn't like, he would make fun of
the poor guy in front of everyone, shaming and attacking
him with unfair criticism. That was his way of telling me
to get rid of him, and I would comply and break off dating
him. It happened more than once, mainly between the age
of sixteen and into my early twenties. At times it seemed
Dean was a jealous boyfriend and he was furious I was giving my affection to another man. Later, subtly, he would
give his approval for whomever I slept with, but if I went
out with someone he didn't approve of the name-calling
would start: slut, tramp or your nothing than a f---king little
whore.

After my abortion Dean was not molesting me as often.
The pregnancy scared him away for a while but he soon
returned. I think the main reason the molestation lessened
was because I was getting older and I tried not to be alone
with him. I know it may seem strange to you, the reader,
but I was always torn; I loved my brother but hated my
abuser. My brother was fun, he was cool and I liked hanging around with him and the attention he offered filled my
craving to be loved and validated. No one ever gave me

the kind of attention he did and it filled the void of need-ing to be special to someone, anyone. On the other hand my abuser was frightening, damning, dark and confusing. He made me feel worthless. Dean was both loveable and despicable and I never knew which one would show up on any given day.

Once I turned eighteen Dean began introducing me to his male friends and often, after meeting some of them, he would encourage me to date them. It became more evident which ones he approved of. I don't recall how the situation was approached but with subtle remarks he made it clear and would encourage me to go out with them. He was giving me his permission. His friends and I were unaware of it at the time, but I believe he was offering me as a token of his friendship and it was also a way for him to continue controlling me. It was so confusing at times. Some of his friends he encouraged me to go out with and others he didn't want me to have anything to do with. It seemed it was always his decision, not mine, who I dated.

During my early twenties we spent a lot of time at the Lake of Ozarks with both his friends and mine. One holi-day weekend we were partying heavy, drinking and doing drugs. I got completely obliterated and slept with a friend of his. The next day he looked at me as if I were a pile of dog crap and called me a f---king little whore and said, *"You'll sleep with anyone won't you?"* I thought he wanted me to sleep with his friend. It seemed as though I could never do the right thing in his eyes. Around the same time Dean highly encouraged me to date two of his closest friends.

Both were very kind to me and they treated women completely opposite of the way Dean did. I never understood how they became friends of his. I didn't know how to welcome their kindness and love, and eventually pushed them both away.

Years later when they both found out about the years of abuse I endured from Dean they said it made sense why I lived my life as I had. Doing drugs, the excessive drinking and sleeping around. It broke their hearts to hear what happened to me and they finally understood why I pushed them away and couldn't accept their love. I didn't know how to process what they were offering me. Their love and kindness frightened me. Having someone want to be nice to me, want to take care of me, didn't make any sense at all. How could someone want me? I was soiled, damaged goods. One told me that when we were dating he had a strange feeling and said Dean acted like a jealous lover instead of a protective older brother. That's when he told me I was the love of his life and he should have seen what was happening and rescued me. Both of these wonderful men were truly disturbed by the truth of what my life was behind closed doors, and like many before them who loved me they felt they let me down.

Many people have assumed the burden of guilt for not helping me and not sensing what Dean was doing to me. It is always sad to see them trying to grasp the reality of the abuse I went through. Looking back they would begin remembering small things that seemed to peek out of the realm of normal behavior between a brother and sister.

Now, clearly aware of what he did to me, they have a better appreciation of what I was going through and why I was so dysfunctional. I've seen the sorrow in their eyes and they too want to punish themselves for not sensing the nightmare I was trapped in. Like others before them none of what happened was their fault, and I hid it from them just as much as Dean did. It is difficult to explain why I hid the abuse, and people wonder why I didn't say anything at the time.

It is not like the neighbor down the street molested me and threatened to kill my family or me if I told anyone. Incest is something so dark, sinister, and difficult to explain. When I was being abused I felt alone, frightened, isolated, and oddly special in my own desolation. I didn't feel I had a right to betray Dean. In fact, I was afraid to utter one word against him. I could sense the subtle threats from him not to say a word and at the same moment ensuring me it was our very own special secret. I felt if I didn't keep our secret he would expel me from his life and would never love me again. Right or wrong the power he had over me completely controlled me, and the thought of losing our bond frightened me. Because of our secret I felt he was the only one I had any real connection to. It was so bizarrely confusing and for many years, even after the abuse stopped, I didn't think my other two brothers loved me because they never tried to have sex with me. I was that emotionally damaged.

The subtle threats from Dean came in various ways. My silence was enforced by the money and gifts, by a threatening look or a snide remark; I knew if I told anyone I would be the one blamed not him. No one else picked up on the comments or the looks at any given moment but I knew what they meant. Sometimes his looks made me feel ashamed and dirty. Other times the looks made me feel special. Not only was I in a perpetual state of make believe and had to pretend my life was happy, but I was also in a constant state of confusion. "You're good, you're bad, you're special, you're pretty, you're stupid, you're a little whore, a tramp, you're my favorite sister, and no one will ever love you like I do."

Today children are told about stranger danger and inappropriate touching. But how do you tell a child if Daddy or your step dad or your uncle or your brother touches you in a certain way be sure to tell mommy? Some children have told. Some are believed but many have been blamed or called liars. When I was being molested people weren't as aware of the magnitude of child abuse, especially incest, so no one knew to look for any signs of abuse. No one, not even Mom, told me to tell Mommy if someone ever touched me inappropriately, even after what my dad did to my sister Punkin. Turn a blind eye and it won't exist. People didn't talk about incest or child abuse like they do today.

I was so screwed up about my sexuality, my body, and my right to say no. After a while I thought every man I came in contact with had the right to have sex with me, to do whatever they wanted whenever they wanted, and they did. I was conditioned to believe I didn't have the right to say no, even if I didn't want to have sex with them.

When I was in my early twenties and working as a receptionist at a landscape nursery I was the only female employee, and there was one guy who was always secretly flirting with me. He would often make statements like he knew where I lived and he was going to come to my house some night and do whatever he wanted to me and I wouldn't be able to stop him. He never said it in front of the other employees. He was careful that no one else would hear him, because he was married. I knew what he meant, cowering, I just shrugged it off not thinking he would, or even if he did I didn't have the right to stop him.

His threats became reality one night, long after midnight. Asleep in my bed, I woke up and his hand covered my mouth. He was on top of me. My arms were pinned down and I couldn't move. He had broken through a sliding glass door. Quietly, with a sadistic laugh he said, *"I told you I would get you."* He was taking sheer delight in his victory over me. He was having what he declared he would take from me. Not moving a muscle, I just lay there limp. Once he knew I wasn't going to fight him he took his hand away from my mouth. I didn't call out for my roommates, Dora or her sister, and I didn't even try to fight him off. Laying there lifeless, I waited for him to finish. After the snake devoured his prey, he slithered out of the house as quietly as he came in.

The next day at work, strutting like a peacock with full dress feathers, he mocked me the whole day and every day after reveling in his conquest. I felt I couldn't say, or do anything against him. I didn't believe I had a right to.

I felt defeated and I knew I would be blamed if I did say anything. The thought of rape never entered my mind until therapy. I felt I should submit to him and allow him to take whatever he wanted from me. Before therapy I didn't know I could or should have screamed for help or tried to fight him off.

As I grew older the molestation Dean forced on me became less frequent. I think I was getting too old for him. He was dating girls younger than me. After I turned eighteen the molestation continued, but only a couple of times. I tried to stop him, but I didn't know how. I tried not to be alone with him but he was very clever in arranging the situation so we would be alone when he wanted to have sex with me.

In 1980 I turned twenty-four. It may have been the year before or the early part of 1980 that Dean called me and asked me to come to his house, alone. He said he needed my help with something big and I was the only one he trusted. I went inside and he was cutting lines of cocaine. He handed me a rolled hundred-dollar bill to snort a line. I said, *"No thanks,"* and he looked at me strangely and snorted it himself. He began to tell me he was working on a big drug deal and needed my help. He told me if I helped him I could make a lot of money. I asked, *"What do you want me to do?"* He said *"There's a big shipment of coke waiting to be picked up and I need you to mule the drugs into the country for me."*

He told me he would pay my way, I think it was to South America. He wanted me to pick up the drugs and bring them back to him. Drug busts locally and around the world were becoming more common in the news, and my life flashed before my eyes. I had a vision of being arrested trying to get back in the country. The thought of sitting in a foreign prison for years scared me to death.

All of a sudden it was as if a hypnotist was in the room speaking to me and said, *"Ok Rena, on the count of three and when I clap my hands you will wake from your deep sleep. From this moment forward you will understand you don't have to do anything he tells you to do ever again. YOU CAN break free of his control. Ok Rena, are you ready, one, two, three, CLAP."*

I began shaking my head trying to clear my mind and really focus on what Dean was asking me to do. Smuggling drugs into the country was an enormous risk to take, but asking me to be his mule was what really woke me up and made me mad as hell. I took his proposition literally and felt he had no more regard for me than a Jackass. His statement snapped me right out of the hypnotic state I had been in for years and I began to have a sense of intelligibility of what our relationship truly was. He called it love for years, but he used and abused me as he had everyone who stumbled upon his path. I was scared, but becoming rabid with madness. I screamed, *"NO, I can't do it! Why don't you go and pick up the damn drugs?"*

My whole body was shaking. Petrified, all I could think about was getting out of there. I was thinking, *"No more, no more, I can't do this anymore."* My mind was being bombarded with the images of all the disgusting things Dean made me do and the horrendous acts he forced upon me for years. I realized, blindly, I had surrendered for years to the molestation just to feel loved by him. I tolerated his verbal, emotional and sexual abuse over and over for years, and submitted to whatever he demanded of me, in hopes he would continue to love me.

But this was it! There was no way in hell, not in a million years, would I ever go to prison for Dean. He started screaming and began to make up some excuse why he was unable to go because he couldn't miss work. All I could think was "Bull Shit!" He didn't care if he missed any time from work. He knew the enormous risks involved of smuggling drugs into the country and he would rather I risk my life and sit in prison for years.

Afraid, I didn't say I would not do what he was asking and made up some excuse why I could not miss work. He kept trying to talk me into smuggling the drugs and when he finally realized I wouldn't he started getting angry. I knew I wasn't going to submit to him, ever again, and he knew it. Desperately trying to stay in control of the situation, he then tried to force me to have sex with him. I was crying by then, struggling to pull away from him, and I screamed at the top of my lungs, *"NO, keep your damned hands off of me."*

We were both shocked by my statement, but I meant it. I was not going to let him abuse me anymore, in any way, shape, or manner. I was sick of it. He was furious that I refused to smuggle the drugs into the country for him, but it really pissed him off that I said no to the sex. He started screaming louder and throwing a temper tantrum just like he had done so many times in the past.

Repulsed by his actions, I knew I didn't have to surrender to him. I felt strong and it was empowering to say *"NO."* He was acting like a spoiled child, stomping around and screaming loudly, *"You don't love me,"* and started throwing things at me. Dodging the objects and protecting my face with my hands, he started shouting that his girlfriend would do anything he asked. He screamed, *"She loves me more than you do, she is more of a sister to me than you are."* I was twenty-four, he was thirty-five, and his girlfriend was younger than me. I think she was eighteen or nineteen.

I stood there in shock, frozen by his strange statement. Hearing Dean say his girlfriend loved him more than I did, and then comparing her relationship with him as a sisterly one, seemed beyond bizarre. Knowing he was sleeping with her and making that perplexing statement made me realize my brother was completely crazy! Dean was a narcissistic psychopath and it scared me to my core. My skin was crawling. Frightened, I didn't say another word. Frantically, I grabbed my things and ran out of the house. I feared for my life at that moment and, I made damn sure, never, to be alone with him again.

My brother was no longer cool and the love I felt for him before he made that baffling statement seemed to vanish into thin air. I spent less time hanging out with him and he knew my perception of him had changed. I was happy I had the courage to finally say no to him. Growing stronger and determined not to be controlled by him any longer, I could feel the bindings of his powerful hold loosening. It wasn't long after that sickening altercation he moved to California. He would never touch me again, but unfortunately, the years of his abuse would continue to rule me for years to come.

11

> *"We don't receive wisdom; we must discover it for ourselves after a journey that no one can take for us or spare us."*
>
> **Marcel Proust** (1871 - 1922)

Shortly after Dean moved to California he called and suggested I move there. There was no way in hell I was going to follow him to California. I had been tortured enough by him. The thought of being around him was revolting. I was pleased he moved away and wouldn't have to see him as often. I would endure his appearance at holidays if he came back to Kansas City, and we would continue our deception of having a normal sibling relationship when we did see each other. It was becoming more difficult for me to act as if I was happy to see him. A storm was beginning to brew deep within me and I wasn't sure if I would be able to continue with the charade.

The 1980's were a complete blur. It was sex, drugs, alcohol and disco. Studio 54 was the rage in New York and Kansas City had its nightlife. I was enjoying my sexual freedom and I would sleep with whomever, whenever. I would pick a guy up, sleep with him, and ask for his phone number instead of giving him mine. It was a series of one-night stands. I never called any of them. I was doing to them what they did to me for years, and I thought I was in control of the situation. I was enjoying myself in the beginning, but in truth I was becoming more self-destructive and taking huge risks sexually.

I am very fortunate I did not contract any serious sexually transmitted diseases. I rarely protected myself from getting a STD or from getting pregnant. I'm not sure if I thought I was indestructible or if I just didn't give a damn should anything bad happen to me. I had zero self-respect and lived a very self-deprecating life style.

I had no idea at the time how mentally damaged I was from the years of abuse. Dean was not touching me anymore but the abuse continued for years in various forms of self-abuse. I suppose it was a combination of many things. Looking back, it seemed punishing myself was the only way I knew how to live my life. I felt I must. Dean wasn't there to do it anymore so I took up where he left off. Being abused and abusing myself was habitual. My sexual behavior was becoming uncontrollable and long before the term "sexual addiction" was as prevalent as today I was becoming a sex addict. I wasn't doing drugs as often and thankful I never became addicted. Sex and alcohol were my drugs of choice.

Not long before Dean moved to California I met a man who was just as dysfunctional as I was. Alcohol and cocaine were his downfall. I fell deeply in love with him and, unfortunately, with both our addictions it became a very turbulent relationship. Neither of us with our baggage could have a healthy relationship with anyone. At the time I wanted to spend the rest of my life with him but we were both unable to offer each other love in a healthy way. We were incapable of living a healthy lifestyle without professional help, and neither he nor I were ready to give up our addictions. Fortunately, years later, after we separated both of us received the help we needed.

We spent a couple of years going in vicious circles with our relationship. We were both abusing me mentally and physically. It was an emotional roller coaster ride. One day I woke up and my vision was blurry and I started to panic. My boyfriend had hit me in the face a couple of days earlier, but I didn't think it was hard enough to cause my blurred vision. I made an appointment to see an eye doctor.

After the doctor completed his examination he looked at me and with a deep sigh he said, *"Young lady there is nothing wrong with your eyes, you have 20/20 vision."* I was terrified and said, *"Well what is causing this?"* He was very kind and gentle in his approach and slowly he said, *"I'm not sure but I think you're at the wrong kind of Doctor."* With a look of sadness in his eyes, he handed me a prescription for Librium and suggested I might want to call a psychiatrist.

The next day I ended up in the hospital suffering from a panic attack and a severe bladder and kidney infection.

My body was shutting down. I didn't know it at the time but I was having a physical and mental break down. That evening a young nurse came into my room to check on me. She knew I was seriously troubled. She tried to get me to talk and, after a while, I just started sobbing. Everything I had suppressed up to that point just poured out of me, though only through my tears. I couldn't offer her any insight as to what my life was like, and I kept saying over and over, *"It hurts, it hurts."*

I wasn't talking about the physical pain I was in, I was talking about the emotional pain from the incest and the abusive relationship at the time. I believe she thought I was in physical pain from the infections and, with Doctor's orders, she put something in my IV and it knocked me out. The next day she came in and said if I ever wanted to talk give her a call. She found a piece of paper and scribbled her home phone number on it and handed it to me. She was very sweet and compassionate and I knew she meant it. The next day I woke up and my eyesight had returned to normal. I immediately released myself from the hospital. I knew I wouldn't call the nurse and threw her phone number in the trash.

I never talked to anyone about the incest or my destructive relationships with men, or how I was living my life. I couldn't even share intimate thoughts with my best friend, Dora. She was married by then and off living her own life. We didn't see each other as often. I didn't have any other girl friends at the time. It was difficult for me to make friends because I couldn't trust anyone. Before therapy the women who came into my life I would keep at arm's length. The women I did meet I could tell were not damaged like I was and there was no way I could let them know anything about me or about my unspeakable past. I would only let people see what I pretended to be. In my perpetual state of make believe I would act as if I didn't have a care in the world, like life was one big party. Every day I imagined my life to be as I thought I should orchestrate it: happy go lucky with no problems what so ever. I felt if I told anyone how truly unhappy I was with my life people would look down on me or pity me. I never wanted pity from anyone. Mom taught me that; appear strong and in control in front of everyone.

I didn't feel comfortable talking to anyone about my problems, and like my mother I could never appear weak. Other people would come to me and divulge the secret battles they were fighting with their families, jobs, or their boyfriends. I knew my secrets could never be shared without judgment towards me so I guarded them closely. I was becoming my mother. I was the one sitting in the chair looking out at my subjects, bestowing upon them all my infinite wisdom of life and how they should live their lives. It was all lies. I didn't know what the hell I was talking about. How could I possibly give others advice about how to live their lives when I was living such a destructive life style? My life was a complete lie.

I met a woman at work who was going through a divorce. Something drew me to her. I'm not sure what it was, we were complete opposites but we seemed to hit it off immediately. Both of us needed a roommate and we moved in together. Cathy and I were actually good for each other. Her life was somewhat stable and mine was wild. She wanted to explore my world and I wanted to explore hers. Cathy married right out of High School and went from her parent's house to her husband's house never enjoying a single life in between the two, and she was ready to make up for lost time.

Cathy and I were late bloomers to the college scene so we enrolled in a Junior College. I was twenty-nine and Cathy was twenty-seven when we decided to go to Daytona Beach Florida during Spring break. After our vacation the two of us, fresh out of bad relationships and working in a sports bar, decided we could do the same thing living in Daytona Beach and have a lot more fun. We were sick of the cold nasty weather in Kansas City and we envisioned a life of fun living near the beach. Another girlfriend joined us on our quest. The three of us sold what belongings we could not fit into our respective cars, said goodbye to family and friends, and three months to the day of our Spring break vacation we were back in Daytona Beach.

After a couple of months I became homesick for Mom and the rest of my family. But after returning home for Christmas the fifty below wind chill factor and ice storm convinced me I preferred the warm sunny Florida weather. I also liked the fact that Dean was even farther away from me. Cathy and I enrolled at the local Junior College but neither one of us completed our studies. Living in Daytona Beach we were on a daily Spring break and having a blast. The partying was fun but after a while we both realized we needed to get back into the real world, and a year later we moved to Tampa Florida. Cathy enrolled in school. I wanted to but I couldn't afford it.

Cathy's family was financially comfortable and her parents paid her way through school and helped her with other expenses. Mom was not in a position to do the same for me and every penny I earned waiting tables went towards living expenses and food. I needed a new car but my credit was not in the best shape. Mom couldn't give me any money but she was proud that she was able to assist me as a cosigner to help me buy a new car. Knowing I was responsible enough to make the payments, she didn't hesitate and offered to cosign the loan for me.

Not interested in school anymore, I went in search of permanent employment. Somehow I landed a job with the employment recruiter I went to who was supposed to assist me in finding employment. It was a fun job and it lasted about three years, until a client who owned a construction supply company offered me an outside sales position. I was enjoying my newly found career and did extremely well, making more money than I ever dreamed possible. It helped my self-esteem tremendously and I was growing ever more confident in myself.

1989 rolled around and Michael, Dean's son, was getting married. I made plans to attend my nephews wedding. Michael had moved to California after he turned sixteen, to live with his father, it was the same year Dean had moved there. Mom, Donna and her two children drove from Kansas City to California for the wedding and I flew from Florida to meet them. It was great to see everyone but Dean. I pretended to be happy to see him.

We were all gathered in Dean's living room and he looked at me and asked if I would join him in the garage. He said he wanted to show me something. I remember glancing towards Donna and she rolled her eyes at me. Once again she felt left out and I could tell she was jealous he hadn't included her. Reluctantly, I complied but followed behind him. Standing next to his workbench he rolled a joint and lit it. He took a long hit and held it in until he started coughing so hard his body was convulsing. He shoved the joint into my hand hoping I would grab it before he dropped it. I didn't want to smoke it but the years of programming kicked in and, like a robot in slow motion, I took it from him. Raising the joint to my lips I took a small hit and handed it back to him. I didn't like smoking pot any more, it made me paranoid. It had been years since we smoked pot together and the ritual of what we were doing, alone, made me flash back to that day so long ago when he took my virginity. I began to shake my head, trying to get the vision of Jesus hanging on the cross out of my mind.

Slowly, Dean's demeanor changed and he looked at me in a way he hadn't looked at me in years. I knew that look and I wanted to scream and get the hell out of there. I was nervous but I was also getting mad. I remember thinking, "Why can't you leave me alone, why can't you just treat me like a sister?" The confidence I had gained over the years being away from him began to disappear, and I started feeling like the sad broken little girl he molested over and over. Why he needed to torture me and turn every encounter alone with him into a sexual one, I will never understand. He had women, all kinds of women, but something drove him to want me, to molest me, to torture me. I was shaking inside. All I wanted to do was run but I was afraid to show him how he made my skin crawl. I knew I had to keep my composure in case someone came out into the garage. I know he sensed how week and powerless I felt to act out against him. I wanted to scream! I hated him for making me feel the way he did, but the fear of him paralyzed me.

Quietly and seductively he said, *"I have something to show you."* He was being secretive and looked around to make sure no one else could hear him. He turned away from me and reached up to a shelf and grabbed a large cardboard box. Reaching behind it he pulled down a small shoebox. With a sickening smile he looked at me, then looking at the box he opened it and showed me the contents. Looking inside the box my eyes widened, my gut wrenched, and I became even more frightened. Staring back at me were the Polaroid pictures he had taken of me years ago. I lunged towards him trying to grab the box away from him and said, *"Those are mine give them to me."* He jerked away from me, tucking the box under his arms, and with his signature smirk sadistically, laughingly, said, *"No, these are mine you can't have them."* He was so pleased with his treasure he said, *"I will never give these up."*

The pictures represented my life and soul he had murdered and I wanted to burn them hoping, perhaps, it would release me from his spell. He wanted to keep the pictures to ensure his power over me. I looked up at him with my mortally wounded expression, my eyes questioning his as they had so many times over the years when he tormented me and they were asking, *"Why, Why do you take such pleasure in hurting me?"* No words were exchanged between us but he knew what I was asking of him through my questioning eyes. He just smirked and shrugged then, turning away from me, started rolling another joint.

The next day at the wedding was difficult but I knew for the sake of my nephew I had to shove the pain of what happened the day before deep inside me. It used to be easy to shove the pain away. Lately it was getting harder to do. There was so much pain stuffed inside me there was no more room. I felt like an overstuffed suitcase bursting at the seams, and it was becoming more difficult to close the latch.

I closed my eyes and took a deep breath, drawing from the deepest depths of my being, and my Oscar winning acting skills kicked in. I went about the day as the happy aunt with no cares in the world: drinking and dancing, and more drinking, trying to drown away the agony and any memory of the day before. After the wedding party I went out with a friend and ended up staying at her house, too drunk to drive back to Deans. The next day, pulling into the driveway at Dean's house, Mom met me at the car and I could tell she was upset. Hurriedly she said, *"We're leaving town right now!"*

I was hung over and confused and just wanted to crawl into bed. I went inside and Dean was throwing a temper tantrum. He was yelling at his wife blaming her for upsetting Mom. The truth was Dean became so drunk and belligerent after I had left the wedding. His drunken outbursts scared everyone, especially Mom. Apparently Dean's fits of rage frightened Mom so horribly she was afraid for all of our safety. I resisted but Mom was unrelenting that I leave with her, Donna and her two children. They were packed and had their bags sitting on the front porch waiting for me to return with the car. Frantically, Mom helped me pack my bags. We loaded up the car and drove off.

I was supposed to stay a couple more days in California. Mom and Donna and her two children were supposed to leave the next day. The plan was for me to fly to Kansas City and meet them when they arrived by car. I was to spend a few days in Kansas City visiting with other family before returning to Florida. Leaving earlier than we had intended, we took a side trip to Las Vegas to help us forget the scene we left behind at Dean's house. My visit in Kansas City was shorter than planned but I didn't mind, I was glad I left California. The road trip with Mom, my sister, and her two children turned out to be a good time for all of us. It was great to get to know each other again.

As we drove away from Dean's house Mom said she'd never seen Dean throw such a fit and she thought he was going to kill everyone. That's when she told me he pulled a gun out waving it around and yelling he was going to shoot everyone. She was afraid for his wife but knew she couldn't make her leave with us. We heard later Dean severely beat her after we left, blaming her for us leaving earlier than planned.

12

When I returned to Florida I continued down my spiral slope of self-induced hell. During the day I put on my professional business face and would get the job done at work. My career was important to me, and to have the respect from colleagues and clients was something I treasured greatly. However, when night would fall I turned into a wild ravenous creature, drinking and partying heavily, searching the bars for someone to take home for the evening. I didn't care what those night-people thought of me. The mornings after, hung-over and depressed about the night before, I was distressed by what I had done. However, within a day or two the hang over and depression would subside and I would do it all over again. I didn't want to live my life the way I was but I couldn't stop myself. I kept trying to convince myself I was having fun, but in reality I was destroying myself.

Sometimes it seemed part of me wanted to keep sleeping with men hoping one of them would fall in love with me and save me from myself. Some men are drawn to broken women and want to rescue and fix them, but when anyone tried to save me I pushed them away. I always managed to tell myself, and them, I didn't need to be fixed and the cycle of self-abuse would start all over again. Most mornings it was a rude awakening, and whoever I slept with would not want a relationship with me any more than I wanted one with them. If we did hang out for a while it was purely for sex and partying.

I went home for Christmas that same year and I was happy Dean did not join us. I had not spoken to him since Michael's wedding. What a wonderful device answering machines are! If the phone rang I would let the machine answer to screen the calls because I never wanted to talk to him again. However, the Christmas of 1990 I wasn't as fortunate. It was only after I arrived in Kansas City I found out he was in town too.

During Christmas dinner Mom encouraged me to talk about my career and how happy I was with my new life in Florida. Of course, I fabricated a lot of the stories telling them only what I wanted them to hear. I did not dare tell them about the secret life I was living after dark and how truly miserable and lonely I really was. Mom was living vicariously through me and I could not disappoint her. I was an independent woman with no children and able to travel whenever and date whomever I wanted.

I dated a lot of men. Some were very wealthy, some married, and some dirt poor. The wealthy men I dated where very generous to me. They showered me with gifts and I traveled the world with them. Those who showered me with abuse I kept secret from the family. I would only brag about the men who were good to me, both the wealthy ones and the single ones. Mom said it more than once, "Why get married and strap yourself with children? Just enjoy your life." I sensed Mom secretly wished she had been able to live her life as I was and hadn't been tied down with children.

During dinner I continued to act as if I was completely content and happy with my life. Mom reached into her pocket and presented to everyone the business card I had given her earlier. She was proud of me and wanted to show off my accomplishments. Out of the corner of my eye I noticed Donna rolling her eyes. Once again, something thrown in her face to make her feel second best. Her eyes seemed to be on autopilot and they rolled at the mere site or sound of me. Mom kept bragging about me and I could see how it was upsetting Donna. Knowing I was living a lie I felt sad for my sister. She always lived in my shadow and I know it tormented her. Mom was not aware that her bragging about me was making Donna uncomfortable, so I immediately tried to change the topic of conversation away from me.

As usual Dean and I kept up the façade, but after a while my bragging began to irritate him too and he hated the fact that he was not the main topic of discussion. He started making snide remarks and said, *"You've really turned into to quite a snob haven't you, with your new career and money?"* Most of what I told the family wasn't a lie but a lot of it was exaggerated. I could not divulge the truth to my family. I taught myself years earlier how to embellish my stories to cover up the loneliness and pain I was really feeling. That day was no exception. I could never reveal the truth of my life to anyone, especially to Dean. During dinner I continued to pretend I was on top of the world and I felt I must, especially in front of him.

It bothered Dean that I was living a happy successful life. I also felt he couldn't stand the fact my affections were no longer directed towards him. He had a hard time composing himself. I could sense he was feeling like a jealous lover instead of a proud brother and it made me sick to my stomach. I no longer felt love or admiration for my brother and I did not fear my abuser as deeply as I had in the past. My feelings toward him had grown into a cancerous tumor full of unforgiving hatred and I could only look upon him as the monster he truly was. He could sense the disgust I felt towards him, and he was mad as hell that he no longer had control of me.

Despite Donna's pain I continued sharing my elaborate stories. I did it mainly to agitate Dean. One story I told and proud of, I often share it to this day. I was one of less than a handful of women in the construction supply business in

Florida. My biggest competitor's business attire was short skirts and low cut blouses. Her sexuality helped her sales in the beginning but the novelty of her sales tactics soon wore off. Eventually I won many clients over with my professional attitude, attire, perseverance, and product knowledge. I carried my integrity and ethics with high regard during working hours.

I shared that it was important for me not to use my sexuality during work like my competitor did. What I didn't share with the family was at night I would use my seductive side to gain what I required to abuse myself. My hedonistic addictions would take over and I would seek out what my mind and body desperately craved. Day or night, I became very skilled at playing whatever role I needed to. Whether it was to feel good about myself or to abuse myself was always dependent upon what craving needed to be fed.

I wasn't aware of it at the time but Dean had a lot to do with my desire to be successful, and he most certainly had everything to do with my self-induced spiritual-suicide. Over the years I became very adept at being two different personalities. Dr. Jekyll and Ms. Hyde if you will. During the day I lived my life professionally, morally and ethically, as the true genuine person I am gaining the respect of clients and colleagues. At night, like a moth is drawn to the light, a force so fierce compelled me to strip away all self-respect I gained during the day and I would commit whatever degrading act I could to punish myself. It was drinking, drugs, men, and I had a mouth that could make a sailor blush. I didn't feel worthy of being respected or admired.

I had no self-respect and I made damn sure others would not respect me either.

After dinner that day Dean continued his verbal attacks toward me and was relentless for the remainder of the day. Once again, belittling me, he was trying to diminish my star by making his look brighter. No one would stand up to him and tell him to shut up, and that especially included me. He pawned it off as teasing me but his words and actions were painfully distressing. I was raging inside but I knew I couldn't say a word to make him stop. I still feared him and I was apprehensive to stand up to him. As the day wore on I became exhausted with his relentless attacks against my lifestyle and, once again paralyzed by fear, I submitted to defeat. When he knew I had emotionally conceded he ended the intellectual battle with his signature smirk. All I could think about was getting back to Florida and being far away from his grasp. Unfortunately I wouldn't be leaving for a couple of days and neither was he.

Mom, semi-retired, was still working part time and the next business day after Christmas she went back to work. Punkin and her husband, Butchy and his family, returned to their respective hometowns. Mom went to work and I woke to an empty house. I have many friends in Kansas City and intended to visit as many as possible during the day and wanted to get an early start. Before I showered I walked into the kitchen to get a glass of orange juice. I didn't notice the front door was unlocked.

I finished my OJ and climbed into the combination tub and shower. The tub had a sliding door instead of a shower curtain. One side of the door was frosted glass and the other side was mirrored. I heard someone open the bathroom door and walk in. It was Dean. He lifted the toilet seat and began to urinate. I was standing under the showerhead and I could tell he was staring at my silhouette through the frosted glass. I wrapped my arms around my breast and took a step back to be hidden behind the mirrored portion of the door.

Seductively he said, *"You know we're the only ones here right now, we have the house to ourselves for a couple of hours."* I couldn't believe what I was hearing. I knew what he was proposing. Fearful but gritting my teeth I said, *"Please get the hell out of here and leave me alone."* He finished urinating but stood there waiting for me. Eventually he slammed the lid down, only to show he was angry that I had rejected him. Once he left the bathroom I dove towards the door and locked him out.

I'm uncertain how long I stayed in the shower. I stood there scrubbing and scrubbing my skin until the hot water ran out. Crying, I turned off the water and grabbed my towel. Wrapping it tightly around me I laid down in the tub in a fetal position. It seemed I was in the tub for hours crying, wishing I were dead. Starting to shake from being cold, I got up and looked in the mirror. My eyes were swollen, and as I opened them wider I got a glimpse of my face and arms. What I saw in the mirror frightened me.

I jumped backwards, looking down at my arms, and I dropped the towel. Beginning to panic, I looked at my legs, stomach, and breast then back in the mirror at my face.

It looked as if I had crawled through a barbed wire fence. I scrubbed so hard my body was covered with scratches from my long fingernails and some of them were bleeding. It scared the hell out of me to see what I had done to myself, and when I picked up the towel it had patches of blood on it. I scraped and scrubbed so hard, desperately trying to wash away the years of revolting filth that permeated my body and soul. I remember thinking, "I wish I had a knife so I could cut my skin off." My skin felt so dirty, and I felt so polluted inside.

Dean left the house and I went to the hall closet to search for cotton balls, peroxide, and antibiotic ointment. I was frantic to clean myself up before Mom came home from work. Cleaning my self-inflicted wounds, the painful stings of the peroxide felt good. I felt like I was purifying my body and soul of the poison that contaminated every inch of my being. My face could be covered with makeup and, fortunately, most of the damage was on my arms, breast, and stomach. No one would see those wounds because it was winter in Kansas and I could cover up with long sleeve sweaters.

Mom came home at lunchtime and she was surprised to see me at the house. Now covered with makeup and clothing, I was hoping she wouldn't notice anything out of the ordinary. She asked why I hadn't left to visit my friends. She could tell I had been crying. I lied and I told her I didn't feel well. It really wasn't a lie! I was panic-stricken at how Dean had treated me, and what I had done to myself, but I couldn't tell her the truth.

An hour or so later Dean returned to the house and I started crying as soon as he walked through the door. He looked at me and sarcastically said, *"I guess I can be a real ass hole huh?"*

Returning the sarcasm I said, *"Yeah, I guess so!"*

Mom looked at me confused and asked, *"Rena why are you crying so?"*

I said, *"I just don't feel well Mom."* She was genuinely concerned because I was crying so severely and barely able to catch a breath.

Wanting to calm her I lied again and said, *"I'm just sad about leaving you and going back to Florida."*

I was ready to leave for Florida, but I was sad about leaving Mom. I needed my Mother's comfort now more than ever. The little girl in me was desperately, silently, screaming for her mommy. I wanted to climb up on her lap and let her wrap her arms around me. Now more than ever I needed her to protect me, to hold me and rock me in her arms, to pat my head and say, "There, there everything will be all right." We were sitting at the kitchen table and Dean jumped to his feet, looked down at me and smirked. He flew out the front door slamming it behind him. That was the last time I ever saw him.

Several days later, back in Florida, I started slipping into an extremely serious state of depression. My self-abuse was reaching a new level of destruction. If anyone offered me drugs I took them, it didn't matter what drug it was, and I was drinking more than a fifth of rum at a time to even catch a buzz, to the point of blacking out. I survived the abuse but I was killing myself because of it.

1991 rolled in as a new year but I didn't bother to make any resolutions. What the hell for? My life sucked! I couldn't see past the present day let alone think I had any future. I felt there was no future for me, nor did I deserve one.

I became a fan of the talk shows: *The Oprah Winfrey Show*, *The Phil Donahue Show*, and *The Sally Jessy Raphael Show*. I favored Oprah's shows the most. I remembered most of what happened to me and I thought, "No big deal I can handle it. I have my life under control." But seeing the guests who appeared on Oprah's show sharing their stories of child abuse and witnessing how their past abuses affected their life made me wonder if, perhaps, my abuse damaged me more than I realized. Slowly, over time, watching the talk shows I came to realize the years of abuse left me ravaged and was definitely in complete control of me.

As I watched *The Oprah Winfrey Show* one day a guest was talking about her child abuse and Oprah started crying. Oprah admitted to incest in her life and I was thinking, "WOW, it happened to her, and she's admitting it. She's sharing her unspeakable secret with the world." Oprah became my hero and mentor that day as I watched her show. She had been cursed with incest in her life and she turned out to be a wonderful successful woman. I thought, "I should, NO, I must, talk about what happened to me if I wanted to have a good life." The more shows Oprah had on the various subjects of abuse the more I realized I did not have to keep my secret from the world any longer.

To begin healing I must get professional help and talk about what happened to me. But the fear of sharing my secret paralyzed me. Mom and her generation didn't talk about such things; keep your secrets to yourself. But I was getting tired of being controlled by Mom's way of thinking. It seemed everyone was in control of my life but me and I was getting sick of it.

My depression grew deeper. I was scared to talk to anyone about the years of abuse and being raped over and over. I could not deal with the shame of the incest or the dreadful acts I had committed against myself. A month or so after the New Year a few friends tried to coax me into joining them at a bar for our usual Friday night out drinking. They kept calling the apartment but I kept hanging up on them because I refused to join them. Eventually I unplugged the phone. I was too depressed. I didn't want to be around anyone. I had no appetite and I started drinking. I locked myself in the apartment and sat on the bedroom floor in the corner between the wall and the dresser. Wrapping my arms around my legs and resting my head on my knees, I stayed in the corner until Sunday morning, sleeping there, crying there, and only getting up to fix a drink or go to the bathroom. I could not lie in my bed, I stayed in the corner, secluded, shutting the world out, hugging and holding onto myself. I felt completely hopeless.

I spent the weekend in the corner of my bedroom thinking of ways to kill myself. With my obsessive compulsions needing everything neat and tidy, my thoughts turned into obsessing about how I could commit the ghastly deed and not leave a big bloody mess for whoever cleaned up. Sitting there contemplating my suicide, I wasn't concerned about my life or my family. I was more concerned about how I should be courteous and leave my body in a convenient manner so it would be easy to clean up. I believe I drank myself sober and my tears turned into pathetic laughter. I sat there thinking, "I can't even kill myself without getting all neurotic about it. Even in my darkest hour, I put some-one else's concerns before mine."

Suicidal thoughts raced through my head. But after a while I realized they were just idle threats and I would never act upon them. I didn't want to die. I wanted to live! I wanted to live a good, healthy and prosperous life. I just didn't know how. The way I had been living was killing me spiritually and physically and I was so damned sick of it. I knew I must ignore Mom's way of life and listen to my gut feelings. I must do what was best for me if I truly wanted to live. That Sunday morning I searched for the number to a local hospital. Their advertisements were warm and reas-suring: *"If your depressed call this number, help is just around the corner."*

My hand was shaking as I reached with my index finger to dial the number. After the first ring a man answered. Several minutes passed before he was finally successful in coaxing my name out of me. Still curled up in the corner on the bedroom floor of my apartment, and crying even harder, it was difficult to speak or catch my breath. He was warm and compassionate and didn't pressure me into say-ing anything right away. He knew to leave me alone and let me weep. I was glad I called. He said they could help me but I needed to give him my address. I know he was thinking I was suicidal and I kept reassuring him I called because I didn't want to die, I just did not know how to live. I pleaded with him to tell me where I could go and get the help I desperately needed to work through my secret. Continuing to cry, I kept repeating over and over, *"I'm broken and I need to be fixed. He programmed me and I need to be de-programmed. I don't want to die, I want to live. I just don't know how please help me. I'm broken, please, please help me I need to be fixed."*

We talked for quite a while and I started to calm down and assured him I would call the number he gave me first thing in the morning. He insisted I give him my phone number because he wanted to check on me later in the day. Cautiously, I gave it to him and he did as he promised and called a couple of times during the day. I thanked him over and over and reassured him I would call the number he had given me and make an appointment to meet with a therapist. My final words to him were, *"Thank you, I don't want to be broken anymore, and I'm going to get fixed. I'm going to learn how to live a good and happy life."*

13

> *"Courage and perseverance have a magical talisman, before which difficulties disappear and obstacles vanish into air."*
>
> **John Quincy Adams** (1767 - 1848)

I believe one of the hardest things for a human being to do is ask for help. It is for me anyway and always has been. Making the initial call to the help line seemed more difficult to do than carrying the burden of my secret for so many years. I wonder why it's difficult for me to ask for help? I'm not sure. Perhaps being uncertain of the outcome, fearing rejection or being blamed for my circumstances. Perhaps being pitied and looked down upon as unworthy of any help. Just like my Mother, proud I could never appear weak. I finally accepted the fact it takes an enormous amount of strength and courage to ask for help. Thankfully, I moved past the point of caring what anyone thought of me. I wanted my life back and I was willing do whatever was required of me to do so.

Waking early Monday morning I was even more motivated to start my journey. I wasn't afraid to ask for help anymore, and at 8:01 am, I called the number I was given the day before. It seemed they were expecting my call because I was scheduled for an appointment right after lunch. Prior to going to the appointment I became apprehensive about going through therapy. I knew there were years of brainwashing, conditioning I needed to be stripped of. I sensed therapy would be a painful process: like peeling an onion, slowly stripping away each layer, dreading the tears that lay ahead. I was scared of "who" might be left once those layers started falling away: who or what would be at the core, waiting to emerge, beneath all those contaminated layers. At thirty-four years of age I only knew myself as soiled and damaged. Was I damaged beyond repair? Who is the real me? Can they help me? Do I want to find out? Will I like the woman who will be revealed from the process of healing?

I was frightened but I knew I needed to be de-programmed. Would the people who were going to help me completely change me? There are facets of me I like and I did not want any of those parts of me stripped away. I know the essential part of who I am is a good and decent person. Being counseled by others I could not allow them to strip away any of my endearing qualities, which are truly part of my fundamental nature. Not sure of the process of therapy, I did not want those qualities I love about myself to vanish along with the layers I needed to dispose of. I am a good person who behaved badly for years and I needed to learn how to forgive myself for all the wrong doings.

Naively, I believed everyone was still in control of me. It was habitual being controlled for years by the abuses, which controlled my choices. I thought a therapist would shape me into the person they thought I should become. I soon came to understand I was in control. What therapy offered me was the key to unlocking the door I desperately tried to open and walk through for all those years. For years I stood at the door to happiness and self-fulfillment but I did not possess the skills to unlock it and walk through. Hopefully these people were going to show me how to obtain those skills for myself and learn how to make the right choices for my new life.

Usually early for appointments, this one was no exception. Nervous, but determined to get the help I desperately needed, I arrived twenty minutes early. Starting to pace, it seemed I waited an eternity and I was getting worried. My mind was racing, concerned what the meeting might involve. Finally the receptionist called my name. I flinched. Shaking and frightened, clutching my purse tightly to my chest, my head hanging full of shame, I turned slowly looking towards the door and knew if I walked through it there would be no turning back. Frightened but determined, I walked towards the counselor. She held out her hand and shook mine. She closed the door behind us.

Offering me the seat next to her desk, I sat down and we started with small talk. Slowly, I began telling her why I called. I started to cry as I began sharing the secrets I had held inside me for so many years. I felt small, ashamed and dirty, waiting for her to condemn me with her words. Too afraid to look up at her, thinking she was looking down upon me in disgust like the doctor who performed my first abortion had looked at me so many years ago. Finally, with her words and actions I could tell I was in a safe place and started to relax a little.

Now able to make eye contact with her, she started telling me about a group program she held once a week and wanted me to attend. She wrote the date and time of the next meeting on the back of her business card. She then opened her desk drawer and pulled out a small writing pad. Starting to write a prescription, she began instructing me to get it filled right away. As she ripped the top sheet from the pad and handed it to me I asked what it was and she told me it was for an antidepressant. Furious, I pushed the paper and her hand away from me. I started screaming at her, *"Haven't you been listening to me? He forced me to do drugs for years and now you're trying to force me."* It was evident I frightened her. Not meaning to, I immediately apologized. However, still fuming, trying to remain calm while gritting my teeth I said, *"He made me take drugs for years, I refuse to take any drugs. I will get through this without your drugs."*

In hindsight, I probably should have taken the antidepressant. Perhaps, perhaps not. I didn't feel like I was depressed. I was being stubborn. No one was going to force me to take any drug ever again. Dean fed me mind-altering drugs for years and I was going to get through this current ordeal with a clear mind.

The first group meeting was Wednesday evening following my visit with the counselor. I was ready. I could not wait to get de-programmed and learn how to fix myself. As usual I arrived early, ready to start dealing with my demons. The room was arranged with twelve chairs forming a circle. I waited until others started coming in before I sat down. I noticed a couple of men arriving at the same time. I became confused seeing men at the group meeting. The two of them starting to chat, they sat down next to each other. A nicely dressed woman followed them in and she sat down. Finally, all the chairs were full leaving one open for me. I sat down, looking at the group of people around me, curious to hear how their story of childhood abuse would unfold.

The group was a mixture of men and woman of varying ages. The women outnumbered the men two to one. The counselor asked me to introduce myself and tell the group why I was there. I gave my first name and said I was sexually abused as a child and I was there to get help. They were all very nice but once they started sharing their stories I kept thinking, "I don't belong here."

Every member of the group was going through a divorce. I finally spoke up and said to the counselor, *"I don't understand why I'm here. I'm not going through a divorce. I can't even manage to get married. I don't belong here."* The phrase of the day, so to speak, was "co-dependent," and because she thought I was co-dependent it would be a good place for me. Reluctantly, the following week I returned. But after the meeting I said to the counselor, *"This is not the right place for me."* I told her and the group I needed to work on my issues of self-abuse and child abuse before worrying about how to have a relationship with a man. I couldn't believe I had to tell her that. Admitting I was correct she agreed that I must work on the incest issues before tackling any relationship issues, so she gave me the name of another counselor.

Once again ready to get on with my mission of getting healthy, I made an appointment. This new counselor was not associated with the hospital I had originally called. She was independent and the only one in the office. Once I arrived for my appointment I was concerned about the meeting. She looked unhealthy, extremely thin and she was not dressed in a professional manner. We started chatting but it seemed like she talked about herself the entire hour. She went on and on about her relationships with men, and I remember thinking, "Who would possibly want to date you?" But I kept my thoughts to myself.

At the end of the meeting she did what the previous counselor had done and pulled out a prescription pad and starting writing. I asked her what she was doing and I got the same response as before. She was writing a prescription for an antidepressant. I told her I wouldn't take any drugs. I was determined to work through this nightmare with a clear mind. All I wanted was to get out of there and I told her I would call for another appointment. Closing the door behind me, I threw her card in the trash. I proceeded to my neighborhood bar and got stinking drunk. It seems bizarre now, looking back, I wouldn't take their drugs but I continued to medicate myself with alcohol.

The next day I was frustrated but still determined. Shaking off the hangover, I told myself getting drunk wasn't going to help me get my life together. I was dumbfounded and upset at the turn of events of my counseling encounters, so I phoned the hospital I originally called and shared my dissatisfaction with the two appointments. I told the person on the other end I needed a place that handles my type of issues: incest, childhood sexual-abuse, and rape. I was given another number and was assured I would find the help I was searching for there. I could have given up, but one of my best qualities is that I am a very persistent woman and once I make up my mind to do something I won't let anything stand in my way. It's my life and now more than ever I was ready to fight for it. I was cautious and upset at how the other two appointments had unfolded, but I was still unwavering and I went to the appointment.

When I walked into the room there were two couches and three overstuffed chairs. The room was the size of a small bedroom, maybe ten by twelve feet at the most. The group consisted of six women of varying ages. Some were younger and a few were older than me. There were two therapists in the room. One was a man and I felt uncomfortable seeing him and sat on the other side of the room. He was quiet and gentle as he spoke to me, so I began to relax and give him the benefit of doubt. He asked if I would like to share with the group and explain why I was attending the meeting. I started speaking as quickly as he finished asking. The words were spitting out of my mouth as fast as bullets from a machine gun. My body was shaking and the tears were flowing as I shared my past.

Starting at the age of four with my brother, then my dad and my step dad, racing through the years of drugs, and then I began sharing that it was my brother who took my virginity not my boyfriend. I told them about the pornography, the abortions, and the rape. Stopping abruptly, I was afraid to share about Dean continuing to rape me into my twenties. My whole body was shaking and I was terrified they were going to condemn me to hell for what I just shared with them. I couldn't tell them the rest.

Some of the women were looking at me with eyes wide open, and their jaws where dropping toward the floor. They couldn't believe I was willing to share my secrets so freely at my first meeting. I became aware that many of them had attended group for close to a year and had hardly spoken a word. They were afraid to share their secrets. I was sick of holding mine in and knew by doing so my secrets damaged and controlled me for years, so I was ready to deal with them. I was prepared to get the venom out of me.

Having watched *The Oprah Winfrey Show* and the research I did up to that point, I realized the only way to achieve healing was to talk about my abuses and my abusers. Lay it out in the open and start working on it. Holding my secrets in was poisoning me, killing me. The women in the group thanked me for sharing and a few of them began to open up and tell me what they were struggling with. Everyone was kind and genuinely concerned for me. They knew I had been suffering for years just as they had. They were not judgmental and they did not blame me. With their words and kind gestures I soon realized they were not going to condemn me to hell. Instead they offered me a hand of warmth and compassion to help pull me out of the darkness I had lived in for years. I began to calm down and knew I had found my safe place, a surrogate home, and my healing began.

At the end of the meeting I was exhausted, yet joyful I had released some of the toxic waste that was boiling inside of me. It was liberating to share and start releasing the pain I had suppressed for years. The women in group made me feel welcome and safe. My shoulders began to relax and I felt my soul stirring. My spirit, still fractured, I sensed was beginning to mend. I understood the abuse didn't happen overnight and I was not going to get fixed in one meeting. I was anxious, but I knew I must be patient with the process and myself. My healing would take time but this was a good start to my new life, and I remained determined to finish my journey. I thanked everyone for allowing me the opportunity to come into their group meeting. The female therapist spoke up and informed me that they only allowed seven women to be in the group. I was thrilled when each and every one of them invited me to come back the following week and my tears turned into joyful gratitude.

I was completely committed to reclaiming my life and I was afraid to miss one moment of group. Devoted to my surrogate family and my healing process, I never missed a meeting. I continued to share week after week and a few of the women who attended before I joined the group started opening up more and they too began to heal. We were embracing each other and helping each other through the difficult process of mending our souls. Each meeting was a form of spiritual CPR. No matter how difficult the meeting, I left each time feeling drained but a little more alive and energized looking forward to what the future might hold for me.

Within a month or two of starting the group I knew I should tell my Mother what happened to me. Mom and I talked once or twice a week by phone and it was becoming more difficult to keep my secrets from her. I told the therapists and my new sisters I was going to tell her and they became very concerned for me. They didn't want me to tell her, and I found out that night a couple of women were ostracized and rejected by their families for sharing their secrets with their mothers. Those women were blamed for the incest in their lives. I was deeply saddened and began to cry as I heard their stories. Their mothers held them exclusively responsible for their fathers or stepfathers raping them. Their mothers, in complete denial, kicked their daughters to the curb calling them liars and staying married to their perpetrators. It was such a betrayal to those women in the group.

I was completely heartbroken and it was difficult to witness through their stories how their mothers' inconceivable reactions towards them affected their healing process. Not only were they dealing with the incest and then being blamed for it, but they were also dealing with the knowledge that by telling the truth they were the ones cast out from the family not their perpetrators. They had hoped by telling the truth their perpetrators would be stopped and their mothers would protect them. What a horrible burden for a child to be called a liar or blamed for what their fathers, brothers or uncles, did to them. Another huge piece of the puzzle was unfolding before me as to why we hold our secrets so closely.

After the women finished sharing their stories I gently assured them that wouldn't be the case with my mother. Knowing in my heart my mother would not react like theirs had saddened me even further. My heart ached for those women. Admittedly I was scared to tell Mom, but I felt I couldn't keep it from her any longer. Mom wasn't the most affectionate or nurturing woman in the world but I grew to admire her strength and wisdom, and I was certain it would be ok to tell her my secrets. Mom volunteered at a women's shelter and saw firsthand how abusive men robbed women of their dignity and their lives. Also knowing about her secrets, I felt certain Mom wouldn't blame me but I knew all hell would break out within our family.

Why couldn't I tell my mother years ago when the abuse was happening? Why? Why? Why? Many people have asked, "Why didn't you tell? Why didn't you stop it?" Well, eventually I did stop the abuse and now I was going to tell Mom. People get hung up on the "why" I didn't tell. In the past when I've been asked, it made me feel they were blaming me. Not anymore. Now I say to them, *"I could give you a thousand reasons but unless it happened to you, you must thank God you will never understand why it took so long to tell."*

The question of "why didn't I tell" is a very hard question to answer. It's not a question that can readily be answered in one single statement to make anyone understand who has not gone through child abuse. It's as though society puts all the responsibility on the child to tell or stop the abuse. Hello people! What about the adult abuser? They shouldn't have committed the crime in the first place. It is a horrendous crime and the abusers, subtly or not, threaten their victims into silence and condemn us to a lifetime of torture on earth. There are a million reasons why I was afraid to tell, none of which would make anyone understand unless it has happened to you.

Perhaps witnessing Linda's reaction to the pictures demonstrated how the family would have been turned upside down. I felt like Dean or, most likely, I would be banished from the family and as a child I didn't want nor could I handle being the culprit of tearing my family apart. As dysfunctional as my family life was it was all I knew. I could not risk being responsible for breaking up my family. It's a monstrous burden for a child to carry. I would carry the weight of being abused and keep silent before I could allow my secrets to destroy my family. Not only was I in a constant state of make believe but I knew I had to keep silent so I wouldn't lose the only way of life or love as I knew it.

Hearing the stories from the women in the group gave me the opportunity to accept and forgive myself for not telling as a child. I grew to recognize I was a stronger person than I gave myself credit for. Survival at all cost! I was my mother's daughter, proud, strong and determined. It is what it is, and I cannot beat myself up anymore for the way my life has evolved. I cannot live within the "what ifs." What if I had told at the age of four? What would my life have been or be like? When I am asked by people who were never abused, because they want to understand why I didn't tell, innocently they push me back into living within the "what ifs." By living in the "what if" it hadn't happened or "what if" I had told is just another form of hell I refuse to live in.

Finally, now I was going to tell. My determination grew stronger in reclaiming my life. I wasn't concerned about the consequences within my family and didn't care how they would react towards Dean or me. If I were to finish my journey I couldn't give a damn anymore what it would cost him or me by telling. I needed to get the abuse out in the open. My silence of our secret poisoned and condemned me to suffering long enough. I accepted my responsibility and tolerated participation and now it was his turn to acknowledge his liability of wrongdoing. It was the following Saturday when I called Mom and told her the unspeakable things her son did to her daughter for so many years.

14

I believe most people want to feel connected to others, to society, and "fit in" with certain groups in an acceptable way. I had been a member of a softball team and a drill team and it was fun to be a part of a group I chose to join. I had many girlfriends during my participation in those activities. After Dean started giving me drugs and raping me I quit partaking in or joining in any organizations. I dropped out of society, as I knew it, and started isolating myself. I didn't feel I could or should associate with anyone or any group. I didn't even feel I belonged in the world and no one else was experiencing what I was. I felt alone in my dark world of shame and insignificance. You cannot have a sorority made up of "one." I stopped hanging around with the other girls and only allowed myself to have Dora as a friend. Even as close as I felt to her I could never share the truth about what was happening to me.

Sadly, because of my incest, I now belonged to a group, a fraction of society, or so I thought. There were other women similar to me and I didn't feel like an outcast anymore. I liked going to group. It was a safe place, but it was difficult to come to terms with a renewed reality of myself; trying to comprehend that my life-story was not unique at all. The details of our abuses may have differed but the suffering we were going through was similarly painful. I hated being a victim of incest. It made me angry! I hated being forced into this secret society none of us wanted to join. We were forced into the dark world of incest, childhood sexual abuse, and unfortunately the members of this sorority seemed to be increasing and it made me mad as hell. Our populace seemed ever growing as stories came to light from the TV and other media.

Most of my life I felt like a loner, I didn't belong to anything and there was no one else like me or no place for me. Finally, being in a group with these women I felt a connection and I felt at home. We shared our secrets with each other but I was too fragile to share mine with the world. My first baby step outside the group was sharing my abuse with my immediate family and, fortunately, Mom and my other brothers and sisters did not blame or disown me. They rallied around me to protect me and they chose to eliminate Dean from our family. I didn't feel bad about them disowning him either. In reality Dean removed himself from any connection to the family. After Mom confronted him, letting him know I told her about the years of abuse, he never came to her house again. He knew he was guilty of insidious crimes but he would not accept any responsibility of being a perpetrator of child abuse.

My family told me they would only forgive him if I wanted them to. I let them all know under no circumstances would I tell them what to do. If they chose to forgive Dean or not it was their choice, not mine. Secretly however, I wanted them to NEVER forgive him. I wanted him to be punished until the day he died. Subconsciously, I thought if they chose not to forgive him it would afford me the luxury of staying a victim. In doing so I could continue soaking up all the pity they were giving me and I wouldn't have to take any responsibility for my part. I really didn't care if they forgave him or not but I was never going to forgive him.

One night at group I was feeling sorry for myself, like I did at most meetings. Wallowing in the self-pity, going on and on about how my life sucked and it was all Dean's fault. I was so miserable! I couldn't find a man who would love me and I was never going to get married. Boo hoo, poor little me. All of a sudden one of the women in our group sat straight up and, glaring angrily and visibly irritated with me blurted out, *"RENA, when are you going to stop playing the victim and start taking responsibility for your life?"*

I immediately shut up and shrunk into the couch grabbing a pillow to guard myself. I was in shock and I couldn't say another word. I sat there thinking, "How can you talk to me like that? How can you be so cruel? I thought you were my friend, my sister." The thoughts kept racing through my head, "After all I am a victim damn it. It's not my fault what happened to me, nor the bad choices I've made. It's not my fault my life is so screwed up. I'm the victim, why should I be responsible." I was incensed and for once I was speechless.

I left the meeting heartbroken. With my proverbial tail between my legs I headed straight for the neighborhood bar. When I woke the next morning I was hung over and even more depressed. I was distressed because my friend turned against me, and for the life of me I could not comprehend what she was insinuating.

The rest of the week I continued to slip into a deep depression. I felt like she was blaming me for the abuse in my life and I was the only one responsible. Alone in my apartment every night after work, I continued to drink myself into oblivion. As the week went on the cloud of depression that hovered over me grew darker and darker. I kept asking myself, *"What did she mean?"* I just couldn't make any sense of it. *"It isn't my fault. I am a victim. He abused me, I didn't do it."* I was so despondent for the remainder of the week I couldn't eat or sleep and I kept thinking I would never go back to the group. I really didn't want to face those people again. They turned on me and, once again, I felt like an outcast. I was angry with each and every one of them. Once again I asked myself, *"Why did she talk to me like that? She was supposed to be on my side."*

The day before the next group meeting I was driving in my car. Stopped by a red light, I sat there thinking about what I would say to everyone if I did go to group. There were three lanes of traffic and I was on the far left waiting for the light to turn green. I was sitting there fuming, contemplating my exit strategy from the group. My hands were ringing the steering wheel. I was so tense my muscles ached and my head was pounding. Completely aggravated at all of them at group, I was determined that I never wanted to see them again. I've never been a very religious person, but the moment I was thinking about telling them all to go to hell, suddenly, it was as if a lightning bolt struck from the heavens through the roof of the car, and the hand of God slapped me right in the head and yelled, *"Snap out of it Rena!"*

Shaking my head, trying to focus, I was experiencing the simplicity of a basic understanding of life that I was never able to grasp before that moment. The clouds of depression that hovered over me, seemed to part like the Red Sea, and the sun was now shining down upon me like a spotlight. I began to smile, and realized I was having a revelation, an epiphany, and I started laughing and crying for joy. I began hitting the steering wheel with my fist and honking the horn. Screaming and laughing out loud, out of the corner of my eye I could see the people in the vehicles to my right looking at me as if I had gone completely nuts. I didn't care because it was all so clear to me at that moment. It was so simple. I was yelling, *"I understand. Oh my God, I understand!"*

That moment, stopped at a red light, the simplicity of what that woman in my group had said was like a gift unfolding. I realized and said out loud, *"I understand now, I can't change what happened to me but what I can change is how my past is controlling me."* I understood it was up to me, and no one else was responsible for how I lived the remainder of my life. I was responsible for the choices I made and would make in the future. My muscles began to relax and I felt a warming, tranquil, peacefulness engulf me. The abuse happened, period. I had to accept it, all of it, and stop living in the "what ifs." My story is absolutely horrifying and horrendous things were done to me and I did atrocious things to myself. But I must accept every-thing and take responsibility for my part. It is what it is and I can continue playing the victim or move past it. It's my choice. The choices had been mine to make for years but I didn't understand my responsibility for making them until that day.

I now had the power to change how the abuse con-trolled the way I lived my life. It's my responsibility, not my family's, not my sisters in the group, not the therapist, and no man was going to come along and "fix me." It's so dammed simple. No matter what happened to me as a child, as an adult I am responsible for my behavior and the choices I make. It's up to me if I am going to have a happy life or stay stuck in the drama of victimization.

I couldn't believe it was so simple. I was habitually liv-ing in a world of suffering and living within the drama. I thought there was no other way to live my life. I hated living like a victim and just barely surviving. I wanted to change how I treated myself and how I was living my life, I just didn't know how. My perpetual state of make believe and living a lie was so repetitious throughout the years it felt natural to live the way I was. Robotically, I performed as if my life was together but continued being a victim and sabotaged my happiness and success. I blamed the world and my abusers for my miserable life. I used the abuse as an excuse over and over for my failures.

Looking at the choices I made vs. the choices I should have made, I realized I was the one impairing my present and future happiness. Anything that could have brought me happiness, relationships with men or women or my career, I made damn sure it wouldn't have a great outcome. Purposely not protecting myself from getting pregnant or STD's was sabotaging my happiness. I made those choices. The abuse made me feel unworthy of living a happy successful life and, subconsciously, I thought I needed to continue the suffering to feel any self-worth at all. I always sensed there was a better way of doing things, a better way to live, I just didn't know how to go about it. I stood at the door of endless possibilities for years not knowing it was unlocked all along. I just needed the knowledge and the courage to open the door and walk through on my own accord. I was use to living in failure, afraid to embrace success, now I could change it all by taking full responsibility for my life.

Sitting in my car waiting for the light to turn green, I stopped being a victim of sexual abuse. I was awakened

and felt as if I were reborn. The light turned green literally moving me forward, but also figuratively, I was moving
forward into a new way of living my life and I felt euphoric.
I sensed a glowing warmth beginning to grow inside me
and I could feel my shattered spirit coming together, closer
to becoming whole. The emptiness I had felt deep within
my soul since the age of four was filling up. For so many
years I felt a disconnection from my spirit and body. I
started sensing my hands, my feet, my abdomen, and my
heart. They were becoming one, whole and connected. I
was embracing the serene sensation; it covered me like a
warm blanket and I felt calm.

My inner light was beaming and it seemed to radiate
from every pore of my body. I had never sensed such clarity of being before. This new feeling was a bit scary but I
embraced it, arms wide open. Laughing and crying with
complete jubilation, I felt an overwhelming happiness. My
light, my essence that had been extinguished at the age
of four, was glowing and I was coming back to life. Now
connected, mind, body and soul, I felt like a woman, not a
scared little girl.

For years it seemed easier to live in the world as a victim.
In truth it was harder and took a lot more effort. The pretense, the lies, and the secrets were completely exhausting.
It has been said your secrets make you sick and mine were
almost lethal. I now understood I was a stronger person
than I gave myself credit for. Understanding by making the
initial call to the help line was the first step in becoming
responsible for my life, and I was taking responsibility by

going to group every week. I had to accept the fact that I was holding on to the drama of being a victim because of the shame I carried and the judgment I feared from society if they should ever learn about my past.

Now I was thrilled and wanted to go to group. I couldn't wait to share my revelation with everyone and I arrived early. My friend who "called me out" the week before was already there. I saw her and gave her a big hug. I almost crushed her I was so happy. She's a special lady. She is visually impaired, but looking at me she screamed with delight, *"You're beaming. Your light surrounding you, your aura, is beautiful and whole. I can see all of the colors. They're so vibrant and glowing. What happened to you?"*

A year and a half earlier when I first joined the group she shared that she was visually impaired. She said, *"I don't want to alarm you but I am legally blind. However, I can see a person's aura. Your aura is distorted, disconnected, and has no color. All I can see are shades of gray."* Of course, at first I thought she was crazy but I went along with her. However, after contemplating what she said I knew she was right. I was disconnected and I felt a sense of muddled grayness that surrounded me for years. My very essence had been extinguished years ago. To hear her statement made my radiance even brighter because I understood what she was saying. I could feel the connection. I felt whole and could sense the magnificent colors radiating from me. I was jumping for joy from within.

I told her I understood what she was trying to tell me the week before and I was grateful and happy. I waited for the rest of the group to be seated before I began to speak. I told them I left the meeting last week infuriated with her, with all of them, and went to the bar and got drunk. I continued sharing how depressed I was all week because I couldn't understand her comments about playing the victim. I felt she was picking on me, blaming me. I shared the details about my awakening while sitting in my car, everything that had happened, and everything I felt. I thanked each and every one of them countless times because I understood what they were trying to get me to understand. I turned to her and said, *"Your words were the most beautiful gift anyone ever gave to me. To speak to me the way you did really hurt, but perhaps you hoped eventually I would understand what you were trying to say to me."* I told them I did come to understand the meaning behind her harsh words and I made the choice to receive them as a gift not as a damnation of criticism. As I was sharing I realized accepting what she offered as a gift was another healthy choice and I beamed with pride.

Our meeting that evening was a celebration for all of us in attendance. The mood was uplifting. Most nights during our group sessions the tears would flow due to the shame and painful experience of sharing our past secrets. There were no tears that night just wide bright eyes and smiles and laughter. All of us welcomed the possibility of hope renewed that our lives would turn out well for each and every one of us. We could change our lives and live happily.

That night we stopped dreading the future and started embracing all of the possibilities that lay before us. It felt good to laugh and joke with each other. Finally, we were a group of proud empowered women, not broken sad little girls, and it was wondrous. That evening I stopped wishing for a better life and started living a better life.

15

> *"Risk! Risk anything! Care no more for the opinions of others, for those voices. Do the hardest thing on Earth for you. Act for yourself. Face the truth."*
>
> **Katherine Mansfield** (1888 - 1923)

Approximately two months after I shared my "awakening" with the group another woman and myself were celebrating our healing and growth. The group held a graduation party for the two of us and we left therapy making room for two others to join the group. The waiting list to join our particular group was growing. Women survivors of incest and child sexual abuse were coming out and speaking out. They were not necessarily ready to share their secrets with the general public, but they were searching for a place to be heard. More importantly they were searching for a place where they could find trust and have their stories believed so they could begin their healing process.

I felt empowered and in control of my life. I wasn't yelling from the rooftops "I am a survivor of incest," but I was walking taller and smiling a lot more. I felt in control because I forgave myself and made a declaration I would write my memoir. I genuinely wanted to share my story and in doing so hoped it would help others find their path to healing. I wasn't quite ready to acknowledge in public that I was a survivor of incest, but I was driven to put my voice to this ever-growing crime. Somehow, someway, someday I was going to speak out against child abuse. I felt it deep within my soul that I could and would make it happen.

Years ago when I told Mom I wanted to share my story, secretly I was glad writing this memoir was put on hold. Watching my hero, my mentor, Oprah Winfrey through the years confirmed talking about the abuse and getting professional help did assist me in reclaiming my life. But there was one more secret that needed to be told and one more person to be forgiven, even though I swore I would never forgive him. Stubbornly, I held on and would be damned to the pits of Hell before I would ever forgive Dean, and I was damned to my own private world of suffering. I didn't understand my stubbornness and not forgiving him was pushing me back into the "what ifs" and back into living as a victim, not living as someone who has triumphed over their abuse.

In the beginning of my healing process I was driven to share my story hoping it would help others, like others who have shared their story had helped me. Yet I lacked the courage to acknowledge and speak the whole truth. I really don't remember if I even spoke the complete truth in my group about the incest continuing after I turned eighteen. I don't think I did. Not working through that aspect of the incest and not forgiving Dean was keeping me from moving forward in my healing process. The courage and strength I gained in the past eighteen years since therapy was slipping from my grasp. The shame I thought I left behind began ravaging my spirit once again. A master of deception, once again I was acting as if my life was "together."

I told friends and family over the years I was going to write a book, and after receiving my permanent pink slip from the construction industry at the end of 2006 it was time to finally put up or shut up. It was October 15, 2007 when I first put pen to paper. Approximately a year into trying to chronicle my life-story, immediately after I finished chapter five, the writing came to an abrupt stop. Sharing the secret that it was my brother who ripped my virginity from me was going to be difficult, but I also knew I would have to tell the complete story of how my brother continued to rape me into my twenties. It scared the hell out of me to know I was going to have to share the biggest secret of my life.

My family and friends kept asking me how the book was coming, and I would reply, *"Oh fine, slow, but it's coming along."* It was a lie. I couldn't tell them why I was stuck, why I wasn't writing anymore. Unbeknownst to them I felt like a scared little girl again. Feeling vulnerable again saddened me deeply. Another part of the shame I was carrying was the thought that after I revealed I was a victim of incest, people would automatically believe I was a child abuser; guilt by association, or so I thought. I would never harm a child, but the fear of people possibly thinking that way about me made the shame even more unbearable. My shame was growing as fast as toxic mold and it was choking me into silence once again.

When I met my husband I was strong and in a good place and I meant what I said, *"I may not be the person I am today had I not gone through what I have."* But since making that statement I was slipping backwards, not moving forward, and I was withholding my final skeleton in the closet, believing I would be blamed and judged. How would society accept the fact my brother continued to rape me after the age of eighteen? How would they accept me knowing it continued? I still felt as though I was the only one anything like that had happened to.

Over the years stories have been revealed concerning children who had been abused by strangers. I noticed how the media didn't judge or blame the victims who were raped or abducted by a stranger. "Stranger" was the key word. It was stranger vs. brother in my mind. I believed who their abusers were protected them from society looking down on them. My abuser wasn't a "stranger" and it paralyzed me. I felt strongly that society would blame me and would not understand my story. I also felt they would not accept the fact that I didn't stop the abuse at the age of eighteen. Why eighteen seems to be the magical number for the majority of people is confusing, and because it continued into my twenties many might believe it was consensual. That frightened me to my very core and I didn't want to be viewed as a bad person.

When a person has been brainwashed by a sex offender, whether they know them or not, the victim doesn't automatically snap out of it at a certain age. Living within my family structure I felt as though I had been abducted from the life I knew before the abuse and held captive for years. Held captive in plain sight and it was essential that I keep the incest a secret. It seemed to me, for many years, the incest was my soul responsibility to keep hidden due to the deep shame I carried.

Because of an abusers inherent power over their victims, whether it is a father, stepfather, mother, brother, uncle, grandfather, or cousin, we who are abused are coerced into believing we must submit and then we must not tell in order to protect both the abusers and ourselves. Just like other victims, I wanted love and affection, not sex. But having the love and affection I desperately craved meant having sex with my abusers. I couldn't have one without the other. They made damn sure of it. I had to tolerate the sex from my abusers in order to feel loved. They preyed upon my basic human need, desiring affection, to get what they wanted.

E. Sue Blume writes in <u>Secret Survivors</u> (Ballantine, 1991) that *"Force is, however, rarely used; the closer the dependence relationship, the less force is necessary. Generally his power is derived from her need for him* (affection) *and often her love. What is left is coercion."* (P-44)

She goes on to say, *"There are several different tactics that the abuser may use to coerce the child into toleration what he wants to do to her. (I intentionally use the word "tolerating" rather than "permitting," because the latter implies that the child has the power to make a choice, which presupposes the ability to stop the abuse. This is not the case, so the word really cannot be used.)"* (P-44)

I personally believe this applies to any daughter, son, sister, niece, or cousin no matter how old they are, before the age of eighteen or over the age of eighteen. Even though I was Dean's younger sister he played the role of father figure for many years. I was still a child to him even after I turned eighteen.

My gut instinct of how I might possibly be viewed negatively by society was confirmed to me in September 2009. I'd taken something for a headache and lay down on the couch to relax. I turned on the TV and channel-surfed until I found my favorite show, *The Oprah Winfrey Show*. Sitting next to Oprah that day was Mackenzie Phillips. I listened as Mackenzie read an excerpt from her memoir <u>High on Arrival</u> (Simon & Schuster, 2009). As she read she described a sexual encounter with her father as rape, and her father said, *"Raped you? Don't you mean when we made love."*

Lying there, on the couch, I was thinking how his statement had manipulated Mackenzie into believing it wasn't rape, that it was consensual. I felt he was telling her it was something special just between the two of them and it was normal for a father to have sex with his daughter. As I looked back through the years of my incest, I realized Dean's actions and words were similar and how he had manipulated me. I understood how she must have felt. As with Dean, perhaps not wanting to disappoint or offend her father because she loved him, she went along with it and agreed with him that she participated freely. Mackenzie continued to read and said she had a consensual sexual relationship with her father until her late twenties.

I jumped to my feet and, jumping up and down on the couch, I began screaming, *"Oh my God that's my story she's telling my story."* I was screaming and crying at the top of my lungs, *"I'm not the only one, I'm not the only one."* I sat perched on top of the couch, turning the volume up, needing to hear every word Mackenzie said. I didn't notice my headache anymore. My heart was pounding, my thoughts were racing, and I knew she was speaking the truth. I could see Mackenzie's pain and I wanted to reach through the TV and hug her and thank her for coming out with her truth.

I knew Mackenzie's words would be controversial but I could feel it in my bones that she was speaking the truth. Many people would not be able to comprehend her statements but I knew she was giving a gift to those of us who would understand her words, and by sharing her truth many of us could begin to heal. Oprah and Mackenzie continued talking and saying things such as "consensual sex" and "incestuous relationship" and I remembered reading the following excerpt from E. Sue Blume's Book, Secret Survivors (Ballantine, 1991).

Blume says, *"The child victim of incest often sees herself as a participant rather than a victim. The term "incestuous relationship," used casually today even by the relatively well informed, illustrates how pervasive this attitude is. Actually, in incest one person is active and one passive, one dominates and one acquiesces. The incest survivor herself often fails to make this distinction."* (P-110)

I kept screaming at the TV, yelling at Mackenzie and Oprah, saying, *"Stop saying it was consensual, you can't say that word, it wasn't consensual sex you have to stop saying it was."* I was going out of my mind knowing many people would judge both her and me unfairly for using the word consensual. Incest is no more consensual than spousal abuse or being raped by a stranger. Incest is rape! Incest is torture! Period! To consent is to be of sound mind and body. I was drugged and manipulated into believing it was normal behavior and I felt she had experienced the same thing. Furthermore, to consent a person must not be a family member, a sister or daughter, niece or cousin. There is no consent in incest only manipulation, coercion, and toleration.

After the show I went to Oprah's website. Mackenzie's show aired earlier during the day in other parts of the country and many comments were already posted about the show. Many positive and many negative. I sat and read every posting. Some people were calling Mackenzie a liar and I just couldn't stand it. Remembering how a few of my sisters in group therapy were called liars and treated so horribly, I knew I must take a stand.

I sat at my computer and started typing and sharing my own story. I wrote about how my brother abused me from the age of four and it went on into my twenties. I wrote about how he treated me like a mistress not a little sister. My story was Mackenzie's story too. The details differed but the torment we went through was nearly the same. I felt I must stand up for both Mackenzie and myself. Remembering my childhood friends Charmaine and Dora,

I wasn't going to let anyone bully Mackenzie either. I have never met her but I felt compelled to protect her, to stand up for her. I was tired of not standing up and speaking out against child abuse, tired of being afraid to use my voice to help bring awareness to and try to eradicate this scourge. I wasn't going to be silenced anymore and I continued typing and sharing my story.

Somehow, someway, someday I knew I was going to speak out against child abuse. I felt it in the depths of my soul that I could and would make it happen but I wasn't sure how. Then out of the blue, out of hundreds, possibly thousands of emails sent in response to Mackenzie Phillips appearance on *The Oprah Winfrey Show*, my email was picked. Two years to the day I started writing this book, October 15, 2009, the show where I appeared on as one of Oprah's guests aired. I had the honor to sit next to my hero, my mentor, Oprah Winfrey and speak out against these insidious crimes of incest.

Not long after the show aired I found myself feeling confused and scared. I knew I wanted to speak out and, I kept telling myself that I was proud I had appeared on the show, but the shame began to swallow me once again and I felt incredibly vulnerable. I didn't feel like the hero I thought I would by sharing my story. I felt frightened, not empowered, and I was afraid I would be judged unfairly for telling the world my secret. There was more healing that needed to take place.

PART TWO

NO MORE!

1

> *"The weak can never forgive.*
> *Forgiveness is the attribute of the strong."*
> **Mahatma Gandhi** (1869 - 1948)

Depressed, scared, and feeling vulnerable again, after several months of crying, I grew tired of feeling ashamed again, and I decided it was enough. I wanted to be proud that I took a stand against incest, child abuse. I couldn't allow myself to slip backwards into the darkness I had lived in before therapy. Spiritually, I was dying once again and needed to be revived. I knew I could not do it alone, I needed guidance to find my way out of the darkness I had slipped into, and went in search of help again. Through a personal educational course I gained the knowledge that forgiveness is not necessarily for the person who commits the crime of incest or abuse, but by forgiving them I was also giving myself a gift. During that course, I discovered that if I truly wanted to let go of the past and move forward with my life, I must forgive Dean.

I stubbornly held on to not forgiving Dean because I thought if I did I was saying that the things he did to me were ok. They are absolutely not ok! He committed unspeakable crimes against me for years, but in order for me to live my life I must let go of the past. By not forgiving him, I was giving him a power he no longer had over me. Realizing my stubbornness was giving him that power made me extremely angry. If I truly wanted to be an advocate for others who have endured incest, child abuse, I had to start with myself first.

I was tired of being stuck in my world of victimization again. Stuck in my imaginary wheel, running in circles not going anywhere. Now this year of 2010, it has been fifty years ago this summer that Dean first violated me. I knew I was being a hypocrite acting as if I'd worked through everything I needed to. I was not being true to myself. I felt like a fraud and I didn't like it at all. I'm declaring the next fifty years are mine and I will not live trapped in my story of being a victim any more. I have a life to live free of suffering, and I want to share my story so others are less apprehensive to seek help for their abuse. I want others to know they must speak their truth in order to free them from the shame and the pain. I now know the only way I can truly help others is to live and lead by example.

This summer, during my class I walked outside during a break. Determined, I knew what needed to be done and I was ready to be free. Just as it was fifty years ago, the day was a pleasant summer day, warm but not scorching hot like most days in Florida can get. The sky was blue, and slowly drifting along were large white clouds of varying shapes and sizes. There was excitement in the air and it felt miraculous. I looked up at the clouds feeling strong and I took a deep breath and said out loud,

"I can't change what you did to me but I can change how it controls me. This is for me. However, I truly hope you find peace." Standing tall, declaring to leave the past in the past, my girlish lisp long gone and able to speak his name I said, *"I forgive you Gene."*

Shedding the last contaminated layer I had stubbornly held onto, I felt a gentle calmness surround me and I felt my heart softening. My heart was opening to all the possibilities of every form of love and happiness that I never allowed myself to experience due to my stubbornness. I realized how selfish being stubborn really is, not only to me but to those who tried to offer their love or friendship over the years. I began to smile because I finally understood what I had been searching for all along was right here with me, inside me. It was me, and I felt peaceful.

During my first awakening in my car I experienced a profound clarity that I am solely responsible for my life and how I choose to live it. But now I was sensing a simplistic quietness, a calmness of being I had never felt before. Instantaneously, after saying those four simple words I felt a stillness of immense peace and serenity fill my spirit. My body completely relaxed, I searched for a chair to sit down.

Resting my head on the back of the chair looking up, I noticed a large bird drifting softly with its wings spread wide, gliding effortlessly through the currents of the wind. I became one with the bird, as if my wings were spread wide too and I was soaring, gently turning, tilting, allowing the current to choose our path, trusting it to carry us without effort.

As I sat there, perfectly still, it dawned on me that in the past fifty years I never allowed myself to sit quietly and enjoy a moment of complete solitude. Always afraid of the quiet and unable to be still, I would turn on the TV or radio afraid of being with only myself. The silence and stillness were not scary to me anymore. They were soothing and I felt happy being with just me, in the moment. For the first time since the age of four, I was now complete, whole, and it felt utterly blissful and serene. I felt in complete harmony with my body, my soul and the universe, and it was peaceful. I was no longer trapped in that wheel, spinning and spinning. My heart, my thoughts, were not racing they were calm. I found myself, I found my peace, and I got my happy back.

Hugging myself and loving the little girl who had been lost and tortured I said, *"It's ok now, there will be no more pain, no more shame, you are free to go be in peace."* I let the little girl go and said goodbye to her. Proud and loving the woman I am now, I pronounced out loud, *"Wow, this is it, my book, my story, genuinely has a happy ending now."*

Did my abusers murder the person I could have been? Absolutely! But to dwell on that holds on to the anger and

I have let that go. I have mourned for the child who had her life stolen from her and I have mourned for the woman who could have been. As with any loss, it will always be a part of me. I will mourn the loss but I will not dwell on what could have been. I celebrate what is, right this very moment. As I have said many times before I may not be the woman I am today had I not gone through what I did, and I rejoice that I not only survived but I have prevailed. I honor the woman I am right this moment. I am proud I had the courage and strength to get through the years of darkness I endured and have come out of it holding my head high. I can't dwell on the woman who could have been, instead I choose to praise the woman who has persevered.

Who knows if I would have appreciated my life as I do now had I not gone through what I did. Would I have appreciated being present in the moment and be able to embrace the clarity and simplicity of the life that I now enjoy? Would I have appreciated that when I am with my husband, it doesn't matter where we are, it is my favorite place in the world, just because we're together? Would I have been as strong and courageous to use my voice and take a stand against child abuse? Who knows? What I do know is that because of what I went through I am grateful for what I do have, and who I am at this very moment. I also know that sharing my truth and living authentically, I am giving justice to the child who was tortured, and the woman who could have been.

When I first began writing this book, I wasn't sure how I was going to end it. I thought about fabricating a picture perfect ending of how I triumphed over tragedy and you, the reader, can too! But I knew it was a lie, and I was being a fraud because I hadn't overcome the shame and I wasn't willing to forgive. I didn't understand the power of forgiveness and the miracles it can create. Now, grateful that I have been given the gift to forgive, and now aware that I have, I can move forward and not just live a better life, but live the extraordinary life I truly want to live.

Writing this book has taken me on a journey of healing and searching for myself. Today, thankfully, I know my purpose. As a speaking coach I want to teach and help others find their voice and speak with confidence. I will also continue sharing my story, resolute in doing so, knowing it will help those who need to know they are not alone and they too can gain the courage to speak out. Happy and at peace with myself, I am immensely proud of the woman I have become. I don't care anymore what some people might think of me or how they judge me. That's their problem! I've got things to do!

I will carry on and speak out against every form of child abuse until the day I take my last breath on this earth. It's not about me anymore, because I truly have triumphed over tragedy! Now it's about the millions of children around the world right this second who are being raped, beaten, murdered, abducted from their families and tortured, mutilated physically and mentally. I could go on but I think you get the picture.

Thank you Miss Oprah. You and your television show helped save my life, not once but twice. To Mackenzie, I thank you for speaking your truth because by doing so you helped free me from the shame I carried for so many years.

I hope everyone that reads this book and who has been a victim of any form of child abuse will seek help and that you are able to reclaim your lives and come to understand you too can have a happy ending to your story just as I have. I'm not a therapist but if sharing my story can give victims the courage to speak out then I have paid it forward.

I vow to continue speaking out against these atrocities and to one day see an end to child abuse. We must continue with these unpleasant conversations, no matter how difficult they are, to bring about change and end these crimes against our most precious resource, our children. Hopefully, sooner rather than later, the conversation will be, "Remember when children were so horribly abused, how barbaric those people and times were."

2

"You must be the change you want to see in the world."
Mahatma Gandhi (1869 - 1948)

The wonderful possibilities of living
and sharing an extraordinary life are endless.

Speak your truth and speak with
confidence, the truth will set you free!

*"It's important not to get stuck in a story of victimization.
Acknowledge it, learn from it and then stick it on the shelf."*
L. Gail Markham